GAMES FOR GROWNUPS

The Key to Successful Home Entertainment

162 GAMES, NEW AND OLD, INCLUDING MANY OLD FAVORITES
WITH A NEW TWIST
AND
UNIQUE, HANDY CHARTS FOR CHOOSING THE RIGHT GAME
FOR THE RIGHT TIME

GAME AND PAGE	TYPE	PREPARATIONS	NO. OF PLAYERS	TIME
Match Jump, 79	trick	none	any number	unlimited
Match Squares, 80	trick	none	any number	unlimited
Match Triangles, 81	trick	none	any number	unlimited
Memory Lane, 28	quiet	pencil, paper	any number	30 min.
Murder, 52	moderately active	pencil, paper	at least 8	1 hour to evening
Musical Laps, 165	active	prior	20 or more	30 min.
My Bequest, 61	foolish	pencil, paper	at least 10	30 min.
My Grandmother, 56	foolish	none	at least 6	20 min.
My Grandmother's Trunk, 111	quiet	none	6 or more	15 min.
Name Game, 17	starter	none	about 10	30 min.
Names, 12	starter	pencil, paper	at least 10	15 min.
Name Your City, 30	quiet	none	8 or more	about 20 min.
Necktie Race, 126	active	none	at least 10	15 min.
Nine Books, 68	trick	none	at least 8	about 20 min.
Nine Squares, 83	trick	pencil, paper	any number	about 15 min.
Nine to Ten, 80	trick	none	any number	unlimited
No, It's Not, 34	quiet	none	5 to 10	30 min.
Number Game, 114	active	none	8 or more	30 min.
Number Relay, 122	active	prior	at least 10	about 20 min.
Observation, 108	quiet	prior	6 or more	about 10 min.
Odd or Even?, 84	trick	none	any number	10 min.
Olympics, 125	active	prior	at least 10	15 min.
On My Left, 16	starter	none	at least 10	about 20 min.
Orange Game, The, 54	foolish	none	10 to 20	45 min.
Our Cook Doesn't Like Peas, 56	foolish	none	at least 6	about 20 min.
Overflow, 22	starter	none	4 or more	about 10 min.
Paper Charades, 49	moderately active	pencil, paper	at least 8	1 hour to evening
Pardon My Pointing, 15	starter	none	10 or more	15 min.
Pass the Hot Potato, 121	active	prior	at least 10	15 min.
Pass the Matchbox, 63	foolish	prior	at least 10	15 min.
Peanuts, 131	active	prior	at least 12	15 min.
Pick a Number, 74	trick	none	at least 8	20 min.
Pin Boy, 125	active	prior	at least 10	15 min.
Pinchy Winchy, 55	foolish	prior	8 or 10	10 min.
Ping Pong Basketball, 89	active	prior	8 or more	about 15 min.

GAMES FOR GROWNUPS

The Key to Successful Home Entertainment

With Unique, Handy Charts

MARGUERITE KOHL

FREDERICA YOUNG

With Illustrations by Phillip Miller

CORNERSTONE LIBRARY NEW YORK

Reprinted 1968

This new Cornerstone Library edition is published by arrangement with Hill and Wang, and is a complete and unabridged reprint of the hardcover edition.

CORNERSTONE LIBRARY PUBLICATIONS
Are Distributed By
Simon & Schuster Inc.
630 Fifth Avenue
New York, New York 10020

Manufactured in the United States of America
under the supervision of
Rolls Offset Printing Co., Inc., N. Y.

For

MARIE AND TEMP DODGE

Contents

COMPLETE GUIDE
FOR CHOOSING THE RIGHT GAME
FOR THE RIGHT TIME

GAME AND PAGE	TYPE	PREPARATIONS	NO. OF PLAYERS	TIME
Acting Rhymes, 119	active	none	8 or more	30 min.
Alphabet Rhythm, 86	active	none	10 to 20	15 to 30 min.
Applesauce, 132	active	prior	about 8	10 or 15 min.
Automobile Show, 70	trick	none	about 8	about 15 min.
Balance the Egg, 123	active	none	at least 10	10 or 15 min.
Balloon Volley Ball, 124	active	prior	at least 10	15 or 20 min.
Barnyard, The, 78	trick	none	at least 8	about 5 min.
Berries, The, 70	trick	none	at least 8	about 20 min.
Big Stretch, The, 130	active	prior	at least 10	about 10 or 15 min.
Billboard, 113	quiet	prior	8 or more	about 20 min.
Bird, Fish, or Animal?, 26	quiet	none	at least 8	about 20 min.
Blow Fish, 123	active	prior	about 8	about 15 min.
Cahoots, 65	trick	none	at least 8	about 30 min.
Camouflage, 135	hunt	prior	at least 10	30 to 45 min.
Car Lot, 28	quiet	pencil, paper	any number	about 10 or 15 min.
Card Flip, 90	active	none	2 or more	15 min.
Carry Your Chair, 130	active	prior	at least 10	about 15 min.
Charades, 44	moderately active	pencil, paper	10 to 20	1 hour to evening
Circle, The, 75	trick	none	at least 8	about 20 min.
Concentrate, 77	trick	pencil, paper	at least 8	about 10 min.
Cootie, 92	quiet	pencil, paper	4 or more	30 min.
Copy Cat, 79	trick	none	about 8	about 15 min.
Cracker Crumbs, 132	active	none	at least 10	about 15 min.
Crossed or Uncrossed, 69	trick	none	about 8	about 15 min.
Eggshell Hockey, 132	active	prior	at least 8	10 or 15 min.
Expert, 32	quiet	none	about 8	about 30 min.

GAMES FOR GROWNUPS

GAME AND PAGE	TYPE	PREPARATIONS	NO. OF PLAYERS	TIME
Famous People, 39	quiet	none	5 to 10	30 min.
Fixty-six, 88	quiet	none	10 to 16	30 min. to 1 hr.
Fingerprint, The, 78	trick	none	about 8	about 10 min.
Five Coins, 82	trick	none	any number	unlimited
Five Glasses, 81	trick	none	any number	unlimited
Five in a Row, 67	trick	none	at least 8	about 15 to 20 min.
Fizz Baseball, 110	active	none	10 or more	30 min.
Forbidden Letter, 103	quiet	none	6 or more	30 min.
From A to Z, 29	quiet	none	about 8	about 20 min.
From 1 to 50, 74	trick	none	at least 8	about 20 min.
Fruit Relay, 124	active	prior	at least 10	about 15 min.
Full Dress Relay, 128	active	prior	about 12	about 15 min.
Get the Marsh-mallow, 131	active	prior	at least 10	about 15 or 20 min.
Going to Europe, 63	foolish	none	at least 8	about 20 min.
Good Guess, 67	trick	pencil, paper	at least 8	about 20 min.
Grab the Plate, 15	starter	none	at least 8	15 to 20 min.
Guggenheim, 26	quiet	pencil, paper	any number	about 45 min.
Hall of Fame, 25	quiet	pencil, paper	any number	about 30 min.
Handshake, 20	starter	none	15 or more	about 5 min.
Hangman, 40	quiet	pencil, paper	7 to 11	30 min.
He Can Do Little, 72	trick	none	at least 8	about 10 min.
Hoop-la, 127	active	none	at least 10	about 15 min.
Horse Race, 164	active	prior	at least 20	1 hour to evening
How Many?, 117	active	prior	8 or more	15 min.
How They Met, 105	starter	pencil, paper	8 or more	about 20 min.
I Am Going to Duluth, 126	quiet	none	6 or more	15 min.
Identity, 17	starter	prior	at least 12	about 15 min.
Indoor Scavenger Hunt, 138	hunt	prior	at least 12	about 30 min.
In the Air, 126	active	none	at least 10	about 15 min.
Jail, 129	active	none	at least 12	about 15 or 20
Jigger Trick, The, 82	trick	none	any number	about 15 min.
Last Straw, The, 57	foolish	prior	at least 10	20 min.
Laughter to Tears, 60	foolish	none	8 or 10	15 min.
Leading the Blind, 128	active	none	at least 10	15 min.
Letter Hunt, 137	hunt	prior	at least 10	30 min.
Line-up, 127	active	prior	at least 12	15 min.
Magic Touch, 73	trick	none	at least 8	20 min.
Match Book, 22	starter	none	4 or more	15 min.
Match Building, 14	starter	prior	at least 3	30 min.

COMPLETE GUIDE

GAME AND PAGE	TYPE	PREPARATIONS	NO. OF PLAYERS	TIME
Twenty-five Letters, 24	quiet	pencil, paper	any number	45 min.
Under the Pole, 133	active	prior	8 couples	30 min.
Up Jenkins, 87	active	none	8 or more	about 15 min.
Upside Down Scavenger Hunt, 137	hunt	prior	at least 12	45 min.
Ventriloquist, 59	foolish	none	5 couples	about 20 min.
Vocabulary, 26	quiet	none	at least 8	30 min.
What Dropped?, 116	quiet	prior	8 or more	about 20 min.
What Is It?, 104	active	prior	10 or more	30 min.
What's a Mugwump?, 58	foolish	none	at least 10	30 min.
What's My Name?, 10	starter	prior	at least 8	about 20 min.
What's the City?, 72	trick	none	at least 8	about 20 min.
What's the Product?, 112	quiet	prior	6 or more	about 15 min.
What's the Proverb?, 35	quiet	none	5 to 10	30 min.
What's the Scoop?, 118	quiet	prior	6 or more	45 min.
What Time Is It?, 76	trick	none	at least 8	about 15 min.
When I Was a Child, 22	starter	prior	10 or more	30 min.
Where's the Nickel?, 83	trick	none	any number	about 15 min.
Who's the Owner?, 69	trick	none	at least 8	20 min.
Word Building, 29	quiet	pencil, paper	any number	about 10 min.
Word Factory, 33	quiet	pencil, paper	any number	45 min.
Word Relations, 31	quiet	none	about 8	30 min.
Word Rhymes, 120	quiet	none	8 or more	30 min.
Words and Pictures, 92	active	prior	8 or more	30 min.
Your Favorite Object, 62	foolish	none	8 or 10	20 min.
Zoo, 13	starter	pencil, paper	at least 10	about 15 min.

GAMES FOR GROWNUPS

The Key to Successful Home Entertainment

162 GAMES, NEW AND OLD, INCLUDING MANY OLD FAVORITES
WITH A NEW TWIST

1. When the Party's on You

THE 162 GAMES, hunts, and tricks in this book have been collected in answer to the current demand for inexpensive, informal home entertainment. Most of us have neither the time nor the desire for elaborate, formal parties which leave the host panting from exhaustion and faced with a greatly depleted budget. But we still want friends around us. We still want to give vent to that urge to "have a party."

Well, games can make a party—a party that is fun and easy to run and costs very little. We will stand in back of this statement because we know it's true. It has happened to us. It has happened to people we know. It could happen to you.

During World War II, we spent three years overseas on the

club and recreation staff of the American Red Cross. Part of our job was to plan and carry out a recreation program wherever we were assigned. It didn't take long to discover that no matter where we were, a game night was a pretty sure entertainment bet. We played games in Hawaii. We played games on Okinawa. We played games in Japan. The rough and tough paratroopers, the fatigue-clad marines, the boys who wore wings, the shoe-weary infantrymen—when it came to enjoying games they were all alike.

We played a lot of our old favorites and then we learned some new ones that were party favorites in Texas, in Colorado, in New England. Whether we were playing charades or a horse-race game in which we rolled dice one foot square, someone always had a new variation, a twist that would make it just a little better.

These men liked the games and so did we. And when we returned home we found that our families and friends were just as enthusiastic.

Game playing is not limited to old and good friends. A very successful party was given by a couple who had recently moved to a new community. They invited ten of their new neighbors and about the same number of old friends from their former home town. Not wanting a half-and-half party, with one group of acquaintances in a deep huddle at one end of the room and the other in a tight little circle of their own, they planned games which would include everyone. What's My Name? (*see* page 10), a game which requires each player to circulate and talk to other guests, was started immediately. There was a guessing game already set up in the dining room. Another one pinned to each drapery in the living room.

Within half an hour the two groups were so intermingled that they never did separate until it was time to go home. Total cost of the party, excluding refreshments, was a pad of scratch paper, some glue, and an hour's advance preparation. They felt that wasn't too much for a party which not only established some new friendships but is still a topic of conversation one year later.

It is easy to arouse group interest in games. One day, in trying to discover the solution to a trick we wanted to include in this book, we brought the subject up in the lounge of a small community club where there were about twenty people present. It is a match trick called "The Cannibals and the Missionaries." We remembered how to lay out the matches, but not how to work the solution.

In a matter of minutes we were surrounded by interested spectators. Match packs were being torn apart like fury and everyone wanted to get into the act. Soon another group had collected to demonstrate a trick with glasses. A man on his way out stopped to show us a mathematical problem. Someone else had a card trick. When we left an hour later, still without the answer to the Cannibals and the Missionaries, the room was an uproar of torn match packs, matches, glasses, and people who were having a wonderful time.

The results could be the same in any living room. It was because we had seen just this happen again and again that we decided to make a collection of games. We have included only games which can be played by adults in apartments or houses of average size. While some of these games can be played outdoors, none of them has to be. And there is not one that requires any expensive equipment or, in fact, anything which cannot be found in most households.

There are some old favorites, with directions for playing them just as they have been played for years, and there are some with new twists to fit the contemporary pattern. Altogether, they represent the very best we could find in games for you to try at home.

There is no set formula which guarantees that a game will

be a hit with everyone who plays it. The game which has everyone laughing tonight might fall flat at next week's party. The fault lies not in the game or the people playing it, but in the combination. For that reason we have carefully avoided labeling any game as "hilarious," or "hysterically funny," or "always a favorite."

You and you alone can be the judge of what will be a good selection of games for your friends. And like most people, you may have to discover that selection by the trial-and-error system. The only rule we believe it safe to go by is the simple one of "Never force them to play, but once they're playing, don't force them to stop."

As a guide to help you in selecting, we have headed each game with the number of players it takes to make it successful and the time you should allow for playing it. The numbers given are the minimum. In most games, you can add as many players as you wish. All of the games can be played as long as your guests seem to be enjoying themselves. There is no point in stopping a game just because you have played it the allotted thirty minutes. If the group pleasure is still at a peak, don't arbitrarily call the fun to a halt by saying "We'll have to stop this now if we're ever going to have time to play Billboard." Save Billboard for another night. It will keep, but pleasure will not.

Change of pace is important, though, and it is something to which every guest is very sensitive. Even the young and the gay can't keep up a very active game all evening. Give them a breathing space by starting a quiet, sit-down game, one of the silly talking games, or a trick you can demonstrate with the aid of a confederate. And if the players have been seated and tearing their brains apart on a thinking game for a long time, give them an excuse to be up and active.

It often helps to give some thought to a starter or warm-up game. These are games which are simple to explain and simple to play. Their main purpose is to establish a mood, to get people circulating, and to include everyone in a game which requires group effort rather than any individual skill. We have put these games in Chapter 2, under the heading "Get Off to a Good Start." These same games can be played at other times, but as starters they do fulfill the mission of helping people learn new names and of establishing from the very start that this is not a routine party, with men talking baseball scores in one corner and women comparing baby formulas in the other.

After a warm-up game comes whatever you choose—active or quiet, silly or thoughtful. Just be sure you understand the game thoroughly yourself and then explain it as briefly and clearly as possible. Enthusiasm is more contagious than measles. If you have it, your guests are sure to catch it. But if you let yourself become bogged down with lengthy rules and variations, your party goose is cooked before you ever start it roasting. No matter how clear your description may be, there is always the possibility of the guest who doesn't understand, who asks another off-track question before you've answered his first. There is one such guest at almost every party and for him there is only one answer: suggest that you all start playing a first test round, straightening out any difficulties as you go. This will keep the other players happy while the worrier gets things settled in his own mind.

Home games can be spontaneous or planned. If you are going to play games which require preparation, these should be planned and set up ahead of time. But there are many games which require nothing more than the mere knowledge of the game. These can be started by anyone at any time. In writing the descriptions of the games the word "host" has been used merely as a uniform way of indicating what must be said or done by the person starting the play. A guest can perform these duties just as well. It often happens that the playing of one game reminds someone of another which he can start. Or it might be that the trick you propose to break a lull in the conversation may lead to an hour of tricks and simple stunts demonstrated by guests who had forgotten they ever knew a trick or a stunt.

The spontaneous party seems to set its own pace and find its own way from game to game, but no matter who originates the games, it is wise to pay some attention to the selection of teams when teams are necessary. Teams of two are quite simple and usually just a "One, two" count around the room will be sufficient. For larger teams a fairly even distribution of skill and knowledge will make for a better game. Pick as team captains people who are familiar with both the game and the other players. Let them try to balance their teams, dividing evenly the guests who have never played before, those who are known to have a particular skill at it, and those who are very reserved or shy. Unless you have chosen a game in which you particularly want the women to play against the men, try to make sure there are about the same number of each on both teams. "About the same" is close enough, for most of these games can be played with more women than men or more men than women. The advantage of having them fairly evenly divided is most apparent in games like charades or quizzes, where some specific knowledge is required. A team composed primarily of women would most likely take longer to guess a question on an obscure sports figure than a team of men. The reverse of this would hold true with questions on food, beauty products, homemaking, etc.

Change the teams with different games. This gives guests an opportunity to be with different players during the evening, instead of having them split into two definite groups for the entire playing time. The only split usually advisable is that of husbands and wives, whose knowledge of each other can be an unfair advantage in some games if they are both on the same team.

Games are designed primarily for fun, not to be a test of any one individual's accomplishments. Keen competition is fine so long as it is group or team competition, but when it comes to individual play, too much competition can mar the pleasure. Games which make a player feel he has been singled out as stupid or ridiculous, or lacking in some physical ability, can ruin an evening. Putting a guest out of the play because of one mistake may mean he is left sitting around and feeling uncomfortable. Some games do require elimination, but when this is on the basis of an individual mistake, we have suggested each player be allowed two or three. This gives everyone ample playing time and usually means that before a guest is eliminated, others have also made mistakes and are well on their way to the elimination point. Too many games requiring individual elimination should not be played at one time. Balance them with games which can be played throughout by the entire group, or large teams.

Many of the same games which you play with ten or fifteen guests in your living room may also be adapted for play by much larger groups. At one time or another almost everyone finds himself responsible for entertainment at a club or organization party. With careful preparation, you can have a very successful game party for anywhere from fifty to one hundred and twenty-five people. The last chapter of this book has been devoted to helping you plan and organize such a party—including detailed instructions on how to play some of the games.

But whether it is a party for a large group or just a few friends, whether it is planned or spontaneous, whether you're feeling quiet and thoughtful or silly and gay—there's a game to make your party!

2. *Get Off to a Good Start*

THESE are "first" games. Simple to explain and simple to play, their greatest selling point is that they help guests learn the names of other players and require just enough moving around and conversation to make everyone feel comfortable and relaxed. Actually, they can be played at any time during the evening. But as starter games, they will be a big help in steering your party in the right direction.

What's My Name?

You will need: At least 8 players
Minimum of 20 minutes' playing time
Slip of paper and pin for each guest

Before the party prepare a list of famous people such as actors, athletes, artists, politicians, writers, military men, scientists, Presidents, etc. They may be living or dead, American or foreign; and fairly difficult, but not so obscure you feel no one will guess them. As each guest arrives, a slip of paper with one of these names written on it is pinned to his back. He must then attempt to guess the name of his famous person by asking other guests only those questions which can be answered with a "Yes" or "No." The conversation might go like this:

QUESTION: Am I a man?
ANSWER: No.
QUESTION: Am I living?
ANSWER: Yes.
QUESTION: Am I in politics?
ANSWER: No.
QUESTION: Am I a well-known businesswoman?
ANSWER: No.
QUESTION: Am I well known for my singing voice?
ANSWER: No.
QUESTION: Am I an actress?
ANSWER: No.
QUESTION: Am I supposed to be an attractive woman?
ANSWER: Yes.
QUESTION: Do I come from the West Coast?
ANSWER: Yes.
QUESTION: Am I well known in the sports world?
ANSWER: Yes.
QUESTION: Am I a swimmer?
ANSWER: No.
QUESTION: Am I a tennis player?
ANSWER: Yes.

QUESTION: Am I a professional tennis star?
ANSWER: Yes.
QUESTION: Do I wear fancy panties?
ANSWER: Yes.
QUESTION: Is my name Gussie Moran?
ANSWER: Yes.

While this is not a main party game, it does encourage guests to talk to one another while others are still arriving. You can set a definite time limit for guessing, or let it carry through the evening, with players asking questions about their identity between more active games. In this case guests do not remove their slips of paper until they have hit upon the correct name.

Names

You will need: At least 10 players
About 15 minutes' playing time
A slip of paper and a pin for each guest
Paper and pencils

This is a game for that frightening party when no one knows anyone. It works only with a group of strangers, but for them it does provide an easy way of learning names.

Write the name of each guest on a slip of paper and pin it to his back when he arrives. Give each party guest a piece of paper and a pencil and turn him loose to gather names. The object of the game is to list as many guests' names as possible while hiding your own from view. Standing with your back against a wall is outlawed, so while you are edging around to see a name slip, someone else will be doing the same to you.

Fifteen minutes is ample time for this and at the end of that period the person with the longest list of names is one winner and the person whose name appears the fewest number of times on all the lists is the second winner.

Zoo

You will need: At least 10 players
About 15 minutes' playing time
Paper and pencils

This is a variation of Names which can be played with people who are already familiar with each other's names. Prepare a list of animals and pin to the back of each guest a slip of paper with the name of an animal on it. Guests then try to protect their own animals while discovering the animal names of other players. On their papers they write the name of the player and the accompanying animal, such as *Terry—buffalo; George—elephant.*

This shouldn't be carried on for too long. At the end of the playing time, the guest who has correctly identified the most animals is the first winner. The player whose animal appears on the least number of lists is the second winner.

Identity

You will need: 12 or more players
About 15 minutes' playing time
A slip of paper and pin for each guest

Another variation of Names, this game helps prevent the men from huddling at one end of the room discussing baseball scores and the women gathering at the other with talk of food prices.

Before the party, write the name of each expected guest on a slip of paper and after everyone has arrived pin a name on each. Men's names are pinned to girls' backs and girls' names go on the men.

Players then try to discover their new identity by asking only those questions which can be answered with a yes or no and do not require any names. Questions on clothing being worn at the party are not allowed, as this would make it a simple process of elimination.

When a guest thinks he has arrived at his correct identity he must go to the person whose name he is wearing for verification.

Match Building

You will need: 3 or more players
About 30 minutes' playing time
An empty, narrow-necked bottle
Wooden matches

There are two ways of playing this game. Both versions require a steady hand, but one also takes a pocketful of pennies.

For the penny version, stack all the matches in one pile. Each guest in turn places a match over the top of the bottle. As the stack gets higher this becomes increasingly difficult and the first person to knock any matches off the bottle must pay a penny for each. The game continues, with pennies for the displaced matches going into a common pot.

To play without pennies, give each guest 40 matches for groups of less than 10 and 20 matches each for any number over 10.

Guests take turns placing a match on the bottle top. When a player knocks any matches off, he must add all the displaced ones to his own pile. The first guest to get all his matches on the bottle is the winner.

Grab the Plate

You will need: At least 8 players
15 to 20 minutes' playing time
An unbreakable plate or a pie tin

The guests are seated in chairs in a circle. The host goes to the center of the floor and starts the plate spinning. As soon as it begins to spin he calls the name of a guest and dashes for his own chair. If the host is seated before the guest grabs the plate he is no longer "it" and his place in the center of the floor is taken by the guest. If the guest grabs the plate before the host is seated, the host must go back to the center and try again with another name.

Some players use a scoring method for this game, giving five points to each player who is successful in grabbing the plate before "it" is seated. However, scoring is not necessary and you may just spin and run until everybody's reserve has broken down enough for a good party.

Pardon My Pointing

You will need: 10 or more players
About 15 minutes' playing time

For this game, the players stay in whatever seats they are in when the game starts. The host points a finger at one of the guests, calling him by name, and says "Who is next?"

If the host points with his right hand, the player whose name he calls must, without hesitation, point to the guest on his right and call him by name. If the host points with his left hand, the player whose name he calls must point to the guest to his left. This second player may point with either his left or his right hand. This is the way it might go:

Bud, the host, points with his right hand at Peg and says "Peg, who is next?" Peg points with her left hand at Temp who is on her right and says "Temp." Temp points with his right hand at Marie, who is on his left, and says "Marie." Marie mixes things up by pointing with her right hand at Ruth who is on her right and says "Ruth."

The game must go fast to be successful. Anyone who hesitates or fails to say the right name of a player, or calls the name of a player in the wrong direction, is charged with one mistake. After three mistakes a player drops from the game, until there are only two guests remaining in competition.

On My Left

You will need: At least 10 players
About 20 minutes' playing time

This is a simpler but far more noisy version of Pardon My Pointing. The players are seated in a circle with the host standing in the center of the floor. He turns around and around and then suddenly points at one of the players. As he points, he shouts—and really shouts—"One, two, three, four, five, Zip."

If he points at a guest with his left hand, that guest must name the player on his left before the pointer has shouted "Zip." If he points with his right hand, the guest must call the name of the player to his immediate right. If the guest fails to call the correct name before the host shouts "Zip," the two exchange places.

This game requires no scoring or elimination of players. While it can't be continued for too long, it does establish names and help everyone get acquainted.

How They Met

You will need: 8 or more players
About 20 minutes' playing time
Pencil and paper for each guest

This is an old-time game that does not need a new dress, for it still produces a laugh and some very unusual prose.

Each guest is given a paper and pencil and is told to write the name of a girl at the top of his sheet. Guests fold this down so that it can't be seen and pass their papers to the left. Just below the fold, the guests now write the word *met* and the name of a man. This is folded over and passed to the left again. Next, guests write the place where the girl met the man, fold, and pass. The circumstances which brought them together, fold, and pass. When they met, fold, and pass. What he said to her, fold, and pass. What she said to him, fold, and pass. What he did, fold, and pass. What she did, fold, and pass. The consequences, fold, and pass. What the neighbors said about the whole affair, fold, and pass.

After the papers have been passed for the last time, each guest reads aloud the one passed to him, filling in any necessary words to connect the sentences.

The Name Game

You will need: About 10 players
About half an hour's playing time

Guests are seated around the room in something that resembles a circle. Each chair is named for the person sitting in it at the start of the game and retains that name throughout the playing time. The host starts a rhythm which consists of everyone clapping his hands on his knees for three counts and then snapping his fingers in the air on the fourth beat. When all the players are going *clap, clap, clap—snap* to the proper count, the host waits for the *snap* beat and calls the name of one of the guests.

This guest, in turn waiting for the *snap* beat, calls the name of another player. When a player fails to answer on the proper beat, he goes to the end of the circle and everyone else moves up one chair. The chairs remain named for the players sitting in them originally and the player must now answer, not to his own name, but to the name of the chair.

For example, your name is Marion, but when someone makes a mistake you move into the chair named "Jay." You answer to Jay, and Mary Louise, who took your seat, answers to Marion.

The success of the game depends upon gradually increasing the tempo of the clapping. When the game is going rapidly it is difficult to keep from answering to your own name and to remember the name of the chair in which you are currently sitting. The very rhythm of the game is stimulating and in playing it a guest has to learn the name of everyone in the room.

States and Cities

You will need: 10 or more players
Half an hour's playing time

All the players are seated in a circle, with the host standing in the center of the room. He points to one of the players and calls out the name of a state. The person to whom he points must respond with the name of a city in that state before the host has counted to 5. If the guest cannot answer within that time, he goes to the center of the room and tries states on the other players.

While the host or player in the center of the room may repeat the same state as often as he wishes, the cities within that state cannot be repeated.

This game may also be played as a rhythm game. The host starts the rhythm of clapping the hands on the knees for three counts and then snapping the fingers in the air on the fourth. All answers are given on the fourth count.

The host calls out the name of a state on the fourth beat. The player to his right must answer with the name of a city in that state. The next player calls out another state and the guest to his right responds with the name of a city.

The game continues around the room. Whenever a player answers on an incorrect beat, or cannot think of a state or city, he is charged with one mistake. Three such mistakes eliminate the guest from the game.

The Smelling Game

You will need: 8 or more players
Half an hour's playing time, or on and off during the evening
10 empty, narrow-necked bottles (small medicine bottles, salad-dressing jars, soft-drink bottles)
10 different liquids (vanilla, perfume, turpentine, Worcestershire sauce, almond extract, vinegar, nail-polish remover, coffee, water, etc.)
Paper and pencil for each guest

This game gives guests something definite to do when they first arrive and it is also something to which they can keep going back during lulls in the evening.

Wash all the containers thoroughly, dry, and then fill each with a small amount of a different liquid. With a rubber band or piece of string to hold it in place, cover each bottle with paper, so that the color of the contents cannot be seen.

Leave the top uncovered, or make some small holes in the paper so the guests can be sure to smell the contents.

Number the bottles from 1 to 10 and place them in a spot safe from the activity of the rest of the evening. Guests write from 1 to 10 on their slips of paper and then try to list the contents of the bottles. This is by smell alone. Picking up the containers or removing the wrapper to see the color is not part of the game.

Gasoline, cleaning fluid, maple sirup, beer, cough medicine, rubbing alcohol, shampoo, and tea are other liquids suitable for the Smelling Game.

The Handshake

You will need: 15 or more people who are not well acquainted
About 5 minutes' playing time
5 to 10 dimes

If you are faced with a large group of people who do not know each other well, a simple game like Handshake will start the guests circulating about the room.

Give a dime to each of five or ten guests, depending on the number of people present. These guests are to tell no one else that they have a dime, but are to count the number of people who shake their hands.

The host then announces that some of the guests have in their possession dimes, which are to go to the 10th, 15th, or 20th person shaking their hands. (The number of handshakes is determined by the number of people present.)

As no one knows who has the dimes, everyone shakes the hand of everyone else, introducing himself by name. Five minutes is ample playing time and at the end of that period the guests having the dimes announce the names of the winners.

Shake the Penny

You will need: 12 or more players
About 10 or 15 minutes' playing time
One penny

As the guests are arriving, the host shakes hands with them and in the palm of one person's hand leaves a penny. "Get rid of this before everyone is seated," says the host. "And tell whomever you give it to to do the same thing."

The guest, in turn, tries to get rid of the penny as soon as possible by shaking hands with someone else. There is no set playing time. The person still stuck with the penny when the last person is seated is the loser.

Profiles

You will need: 10 or more players
Half an hour's playing time
A sheet of 8½ x 11 paper for each guest
Pins
A lamp
Pencil and paper for each guest

As each guest arrives, stand him sideways close to the wall and place a lamp on the other side of him, so that his profile casts a shadow on the wall. Then hold a sheet of paper on the wall and draw around the shadow of his profile. Number each sheet on the front and write the guest's name on the back of the paper.

As soon as you have each player's profile, pin the drawings to a drapery. Each player is provided with pencil and paper and attempts to identify each numbered profile with one of the guests.

This is a good starter game because in order to identify the profiles each guest has to learn every other player's name.

When I Was a Child

You will need: 10 or more players
Half an hour's playing time
A baby picture of each guest
Pencil and paper for each guest
Paper clips

Ask each guest to bring a baby picture, or the earliest picture he has of himself. Clip a number on each one of these and arrange them in gallery fashion around the room.

Guests number their slips and then try to fill in the name of each baby.

Match Book

You will need: 4 or more players
15 minutes' playing time
A book of matches for each guest

Match Book sounds like a very simple game. The host merely asks a guest to light every match in the book in rapid succession and on the first strike. He must also extinguish each match with his first blow. Players usually set about this with a feeling of easy accomplishment but soon discover that lighting and extinguishing each match on the first attempt is quite difficult.

Overflow

You will need: 4 or more players
10 minutes' playing time
A small glass

Fill a small glass with water until it is almost brimming over. Guests take turns sliding a penny into the glass. It takes more pennies than you would think to make the water spill over the edge. The guests are to guess how many pennies can be dropped in before the water overflows.

The Spider Web

You will need: At least 10 or 12 players
About 20 minutes' playing time
A spool of heavy thread or twine for each guest

This game is started practically as soon as the guests are inside the front door. Each one is handed a wooden spool with a short length of heavy thread or twine already rolled on it. The guests are told to wind up the rest of the thread without getting any knots in it. The thread is wound under rugs and around furniture, bannisters, lamps, etc. The first one to get to the end and find a slip of paper reading THE END is the winner.

3. For the Quiet Type

GAMES of thought, most of these can be played sitting down. But sitting or not, they require individual rather than group or team effort. You may make them as simple or as difficult as you wish, depending on the interests and desires of your guests.

Twenty-five Letters

You will need: Any number of players
About 45 minutes' playing time
A sheet of paper and a pencil for each player

Each guest is given a piece of paper on which he draws a

square and then divides this into twenty-five small squares—five small horizontal boxes and five vertical ones. One of the players calls out a letter at random and each guest puts it in one of the small squares. Then the next one calls a letter, the next, and the next.

The object of the game is for each individual to place these letters in the squares so that they will make as many different words as possible. The words may be either horizontal or vertical. The same letter may be called more than once and the calling continues until 25 letters have been called.

Proper names do not count and the letters spelling words must be consecutively arranged in the squares. Also, short words within longer ones do not add to the points. As for example: SHINE cannot count as IN and SHIN as well as SHINE. Five points are given for a five-letter word, three points for a word of four letters, and one point for a word of three letters. Two-letter words do not count as points.

Hall of Fame

You will need: Any number of players
About half an hour's playing time
Pencil and paper for each guest

A letter is suggested, time is kept, and everybody puts down as many names, first or last, beginning with this letter as he can remember. It may be a general list, made up of all well-known people, or you may concentrate on athletes, movie stars, politicians, writers, etc., depending on the interests of your guests.

Vocabulary

You will need: At least 8 players
About a half hour's playing time

The host thinks of a word and gives the first letter of his word. The next player thinks of a word beginning with this letter and gives the second letter. The third player thinks of a word that begins with the first two letters and gives the third letter. The object of the game is to avoid completing a word. When a player has completed three words, or fails to think of a word which begins with the letters already mentioned, he is dropped from the game. A person can be challenged for an impossible word and if proven wrong is charged with having completed a word.

Bird, Fish, or Animal?

You will need: At least 8 players
About 20 minutes' playing time

Guests are seated around the room with one in the middle of the floor. He points at one of the seated guests and says "Bird, fish, or animal" and then says one of these again; for example, "Bird." The guest quickly thinks of a kind of bird before the person pointing counts 10. If he doesn't think of one, he must go to the center and try to catch someone else.

Guggenheim

You will need: Any number of players
About 45 minutes' playing time
Pencil and paper for each guest

First of all, five or six categories are selected, such as capital cities in the United States; names of politicians, movie stars, football or baseball players, books, military leaders, cities, automobiles, etc. Then a word with five or six letters is chosen, preferably without too many vowels and without a double letter. PLANT, STAND, WRONG, THIRD, THINK, BLACK are examples of words that may be used.

	STATE CAPITOLS	COUNTRIES	MOVIE STARS	BOOKS	FLOWERS
S	SACRAMENTO, CALIF.	SALVADOR	GEORGE SANDERS	SEVEN STOREY MOUNTAIN	SWEET PEA
T	TRENTON, NEW JERSEY	TURKEY	SPENCER TRACY	THEIR FINEST HOUR	TULIP
A	ATLANTA, GEORGIA	AUSTRIA	DON AMECHE	THE ADVENTURER	ASTER
N	NASHVILLE, TENN.	NETHER-LANDS	DAVID NIVEN	NIGHT-RUNNERS OF BENGAL	NARCISSUS
D	DENVER, COLO.	DENMARK	DORIS DAY	THE DISENCHANTED	DAFFODIL

The papers are blocked off in squares with the categories written in each of the squares across the top, eliminating the top left one. The chosen word is written in the vertical squares, leaving the top one blank. A time limit should be agreed upon.

The object of the game is to fill in the spaces using the letters on the left as first letters for the categories at the top of the box. Before you begin you should make it clear that words such as *a, the, an, and, of,* and *in* do not count as first words; that in answers of two words the first letter of the first word is the one that counts, and in proper names the first letter of the last name.

It's best for your score if you can think of unusual answers. This is the way the scoring goes: if you have a correct answer and no one else has the same, you are given five points; if two people have it, three points; if three people have it, one point. If more than three people have it, there is no score. When you can think of the answer in the form of a double letter—for example, a play could be "Peter Pan" under *P*, you receive 10 points if no one else has thought of the same thing. If another person has it, you receive five points.

Memory Lane

You will need: Any number of players
About half an hour's playing time
Pencil and paper for each guest

This memory game would be appropriate only for a group of people who are familiar with the same residential or business section. One of the guests picks out a certain block, either of stores or houses. and asks everyone to write down the order, by store or family name, in which they come on a certain side of the street. It solves a few arguments if the lists have been checked beforehand by the person giving the problem.

The Car Lot

You will need: Any number of players
About 10 or 15 minutes' playing time
Pencil and paper for each

This is a variation of Memory Lane which can be used for a car-happy group. The object is to make a list of all the automobiles you have ever heard of, obsolete, foreign, and on the market. The playing time should not be more than 15 minutes and the person with the longest list of actual cars, past or present, is the winner.

Word Building

You will need: Any number of players
Five minutes for each word
Pencil and paper for each

A word such as "heart" is chosen and the guests are asked to make a list of simple or compound words which include the key word "heart." For example: heartache, heartbeat, heart-block, heartburn, heart disease, hearten, heartfelt, heart-free, heartless, heartrending, heartstrings, heartthrob, heartblood, heartbreaker, heartgrief, heartiness, heartless, heartlike, heartsick, hearty, etc. Other good key words are: strong, water, weak, thick, thunder, self, etc.

When the five minutes are up the lists are read individually and each person crosses out any of his words that also appear on the list of another player. Each word not on another list scores five points. If nobody has a word not used by any of the others, the winner is the person with the longest list. The list must be composed of good English words, their definitions must be known by the people who use them, and any impossible word can be challenged.

From A to Z

You will need: About 8 players
About 20 minutes' playing time

The guests are seated around the room and the one who starts the game says "I am going on a trip and will take with me an atlas," or anything else that begins with an *A*. The player on his left repeats what he has said and adds something that begins with *B,* for example, baggage. Then the next guest repeats what the first two have said and adds a word that begins with a *C,* like cats. The next person says "I am going on a trip and will take with me an atlas, baggage, cats" and then adds his own word, beginning with a *D.* This goes on as long as each guest can remember and quote what each person has said before him. A point is charged against each one who cannot quote correctly, or cannot think of something beginning with his letter.

A variation of this game is to play it the same way except to use cities. For instance, "I am going on a tour and will visit Athens." The next person might say, "I am going on a tour and will visit Athens and Boston," etc. This version is particularly appropriate for the geography-minded.

Name Your City

You will need: Eight or more players
About 20 minutes' playing time

This game starts with one of the guests naming a city and then spelling it. The person on his left names another city that begins with the last letter of the first city mentioned. The next one names and spells a city that starts with the last letter of the second city.

For instance, the first guest might say Oshkosh, O-S-H-K-O-S-H. The person on his left would pick up the last H of Oshkosh and say Harrison, H-A-R-R-I-S-O-N. The third one around would use the N in Harrison and say New Orleans, N-E-W O-R-L-E-A-N-S, and so on around the room. If one of the guests makes three mistakes by not being able to think of a place quickly enough, or spells it incorrectly, he is out of the game.

If there are more than eight or ten guests playing, it adds

to the fun to divide them into two teams. When the game is played this way, the first player of one team names and spells a city; the first player of the second team picks up the last letter for the first one of his city. The second player of the first team would spell the next one, the second player of the second team would follow. The winning team is the one that makes the fewest mistakes.

Word Relations

You will need: About 8 players
Half an hour's playing time

The best way to get through this game is to make your mind as blank as possible and let your "stream of consciousness" do the rest. This is the way it goes. The guest who starts picks up any word at random. He might say "road." The person on his left thinks of another word that is suggested by road, perhaps "concrete." The third guest might think of "mixer." The next one "cake," the next "chocolate," the next "bar," the next "cocktail," and around the circle it goes.

After it has gone around several times, the starter says "Reverse." Then the last person to name a word must remember the word said by the guest before him, and back around the circle it goes—"cocktail," "bar," "chocolate," "cake," "mixer," "concrete," "road." The chances are, though, that it won't get all the way around without someone hesitating too long or saying the wrong word. In this case, if you have enough players to continue playing, he is out of the game. If the group is too small for this, the player who makes a mistake gets a black mark and the final winner is the one who receives the fewest marks against him.

Expert

You will need: About 8 players
Half an hour's playing time

There is great variety to this game, depending on the interests of your guests. The host starts the questioning. He may use movie stars and movies as the subject if the gathering is Hollywood-conscious. If so, he would say "I am going to the movies tomorrow and will see so-and-so in such-and-such a picture" and he would name a star and a picture. Then he would question each of the guests by asking questions about the star and the picture such as:

"Is the star a comedian?" "Who produced the picture?" "Is she a redhead?" "Who is the leading man?" "What is the location of the final scene?" "Who is the star's husband?" "How many children does she have?" "Where is the movie playing?"

As each person answers a question correctly he is given a match, a chip, or stage money. When everyone has had a turn being the questioner, the money is counted to find out who has answered the most questions correctly.

The leader might pick a city of interest and go around the room with questions about this city, asking:

"In what state or country is this city?" "What is its population?" "For what is it most noted?" "How far is it from where we are now?" "Did it go Republican or Democratic in the last election?"

Questions may be asked also about a certain book and its author, about a sport or a particular athlete, about the stock market, about a politician.

Word Factory

You will need: Any number of players
About 45 minutes' playing time
Pencil and paper for each

A word is decided on by one of the players and written at the top of each sheet of paper. The object of the game is for each individual to find in a given time as many words as possible using the letters of the chosen word. If *characteristic* were the word, some of the words that would come out of it are: charter, car, teach, this, that, hat, hit, ear, are, artist, itch, reach, etc.

Any word that has at least 10 or 12 letters and 3 or 4 vowels in it makes a good key word. Productive, kleptomaniac, humidification, forementioned, disaccordance, blunderhead, retrospection are good examples. The guest with the longest list of English words is the winner. Proper names are not counted.

The Three W's

You will need: At least 8 players
About half an hour's playing time

One of the guests leaves the room and the rest of the group decide on one person, place, or thing. When he returns to the room he must guess what noun they have in mind by asking questions beginning with when, why, and where. The game continues until the guesser gets the right answer or gives up; then the next person leaves the room.

If the article chosen were a lipstick the questions and answers might be:

QUESTION: When do you like it?
ANSWER: Most of the time.

QUESTION: Why do you like it?
ANSWER: Because it makes me look better.
QUESTION: Where do you like it?
ANSWER: On my face.

The player guessing asks these same questions of the other guests. Their answers must be different each time.

No, It's Not

You will need: 5 to 10 players
At least half an hour's playing time

No, It's Not is a difficult version of Twenty Questions. Designed to make everyone think, it requires general knowledge and gets everyone into the game.

One player goes into another room while the rest of the group decide on the name of a person or place he must identify by means of twenty direct questions which can be answered by Yes or No.

When a name has been agreed upon, he returns and starting with the first player on his left, asks each a question in turn.

All answers begin with yes or no, but must be followed by a name starting with the first letter of the selected word. Assuming the living-room group has decided on the name Flagstad (Kirsten), the game might go something like this:

QUESTION: Is it a country?
1ST PLAYER: No, it is not France.
QUESTION: Is it a man?
2ND PLAYER: No, it is not Franco.
QUESTION: Is it a city?
3RD PLAYER: No, it is not Florence.
QUESTION: Is it a state?
4TH PLAYER: No, it is not Florida.

QUESTION: Is it a woman?
5TH PLAYER: Yes, but it is not Arline Francis.
QUESTION: Is it a woman author?
6TH PLAYER: No, it is not Edna Ferber.

The questioner continues until he guesses the correct answer or has exhausted his twenty questions. He gets ten points if he guesses the answer and has ten charged against him if he fails to do so. A player who cannot answer the question by filling in the name of a similar person or place with the same first letter has two points charged against him.

What's the Proverb?

You will need: 5 to 10 players
At least half an hour's playing time

Just as in No, It's Not, this game puts a good deal of the burden on the players as well as the person asking the questions. One player goes into another room while the remaining guests decide on a proverb. When the questioner returns, he is told how many words are in the selected proverb and that he must discover the proverb by asking questions of each player in turn.

The first player must include the first word of the proverb in his answer. The second player is responsible for the second word, etc. In this game articles and conjunctions such as *and, a, the,* etc. count as words. As a rule long proverbs are more difficult than short ones, but if the players bury their proverb word in a sensible-sounding sentence, a questioner may have trouble with a three-word proverb.

Using the proverb "Home is where the heart is," the question session might go like this:

QUESTIONER (who has been told there are six words): Does this proverb have anything to do with love?

1ST PLAYER: Well, it never really mentions the word love, but it does mention two things that might be called the *home* or very center of love.

QUESTIONER: Is it about marriage?

2ND PLAYER: Marriage *is* not one of the words in this proverb.

QUESTIONER: Is it about children?

3RD PLAYER: It is about places *where* children might be.

Etc.

The questioner is entitled to two questions for every word in the proverb.

Proverb Ball

You will need: 5 to 10 players
15 minutes' to half an hour's playing time
A small, soft object such as a rolled-up handkerchief, toy, or package of cigarettes

This is a game for short-time playing only, for even the nimble-witted soon run out of proverbs. Players may stay seated or form a circle. The player holding the cigarette pack suddenly throws it to another player and starts to count to ten. The player catching it must quote a proverb before the thrower reaches 10. If he can do this he throws the pack. If not, it is returned to the first player, who tries throwing it to someone else. The same proverb cannot be repeated, which gives the game a short life. However, it is good for spur-of-the-moment playing.

PROVERBS

A bird in the hand is worth two in the bush.

A cat has nine lives.

A fool and his money are soon parted.

A friend in need is a friend indeed.

A guilty conscience needs no accuser.

A little man may cast a great shadow.

A man is known by the company he keeps.

A penny saved is a penny got.

A stitch in time saves nine.

A rolling stone gathers no moss.

A thing is bigger for being shared.

Actions speak louder than words.

All are not hanged that are condemned.

All's fair in love and war.

Any port in a storm.

Blood is thicker than water.

Dead men tell no tales.

Early to bed and early to rise makes a man healthy, wealthy, and wise.

Every cloud has a silver lining.

Every dog has his day.

Everything comes to those who wait.

Forewarned is forearmed.

God helps those who help themselves.

Good fortune is never good till it is lost.

He laughs best that laughs last.

Great haste makes great waste.

Honesty is the best policy.

If wishes were horses, beggars might ride.

Ill-doers are ill-thinkers.

It is better to be happy than wise.

It is no use to cry over spilt milk.

It takes two to make a quarrel.

Let sleeping dogs lie.

Like father, like son.

Live and learn.

Look before you leap.

Many hands make light work.

Necessity is the mother of invention.

Three Guesses

You will need: 5 to 10 players
Half an hour's playing time

The host announces he has decided on the name of some famous person which the guests must determine by asking three questions each. These need not be answered by yes or no only and players need not ask their three all at once. The guest who has used his three questions without guessing correctly is eliminated from the game. The player guessing correctly selects the next famous person.

If the host has chosen Abraham Lincoln, the questioning might be like this:

1ST PLAYER: Are you living or dead?
HOST: Dead.
2ND PLAYER: Are you a man or a woman?
HOST: Man.
3RD PLAYER: Are you famous in literature or history?
HOST: History.
5TH PLAYER: In American history or that of another country?
HOST: American history.
2ND PLAYER: Were you famous as a general, a statesman, or a writer?
HOST: Statesman.
4TH PLAYER: Were you ever President?
HOST: Yes.

Etc.

Famous People

You will need: 5 to 10 players
Half an hour's playing time

The host selects a famous person and endeavors to give as many facts about him as he can without having the guests guess his name. Players may guess a name after each fact is given, and the one who guesses correctly selects a name for the next round. Players keep their own scores and the winner is the person who can list the most facts before the famous character is named. Selection of the name is very important, because the more obscure or unknown facts you can think of, the greater are your chances of having the longest list of facts.

If the host selects George Washington as a name, he might list the following facts:

1. I was born in Virginia in the eighteenth century.
2. I married a very wealthy widow.
3. Once I fought on the side of the British and later against them.
4. I rose from being a surveyor of land to being a land owner.
5. I was chairman of the Constitutional Convention.

Etc.

Hangman

You will need: 7 to 11 players
Half an hour's playing time
Large sheets of paper marked into 4 squares
Pencils

This is a game which has been a favorite for 2 players, and which has now been adapted for teams of 3, 4, or 5 players each.

Establish the teams in two separate rooms, or at opposite ends of the room. The host, who has made up a list of words to be spelled, takes his station at a point midway between the two teams.

The first player of each team goes to the host and receives the word to be spelled. Racing back to his group, he draws a hangman's stand in the first box on one of the large sheets of paper and then just below it a small dash for each letter of the word. His teammates guess a letter. If this letter appears in the word one or more times, he writes it in the proper blanks. If it does not, he draws a circle for a head in the noose and the team is on its way to be hanged. A team has six incorrect guesses (one for the head, one for the body, one for each arm and leg) before being hanged.

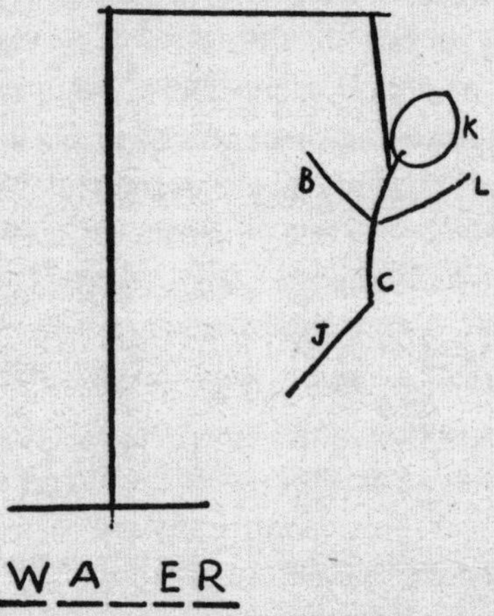

As soon as they have guessed the word, the second player runs to the host for the next word. If they are hanged before getting the right word, the first player must go to the host, report the hanging, and return to his seat before the next player can go get his word. The game continues until the host's list has been completed.

Each team receives ten points for every correctly guessed word and a bonus of twenty points goes to the team finishing first.

The game may also be played with one guest trying to hang the rest of the group.

Teapot

You will need: 6 or more players
Half an hour's playing time

One player leaves the room while the others select two words that sound alike when spoken, but have different meanings, such as role (a part in a play or movie) and roll (bread).

The missing player is recalled to the room and told that he may ask questions (of any player and in no particular order) in trying to determine the selected words. The other guests will answer his questions in such a way as always to include the word *teapot* as a substitute for the word to be guessed.

The questions and answers might be:

QUESTIONER: Dick, what would the newspapers say about this word?

DICK: Why I just read that Lana Turner has a terrific new teapot.

QUESTIONER: Do you have a terrific teapot, Helen?

HELEN: Not any more. I ate my teapot for breakfast.

QUESTIONER: Dick, you said Lana Turner has one. Will she eat her teapot for breakfast?

DICK: I don't know about her breakfast at all. I think this is her first teapot in quite a while though.

QUESTIONER: How about you, Joan, have you ever had a teapot, one you can't eat, I mean?

JOAN: Yes, I had a small teapot once but I wasn't very good in it. It wasn't my kind of teapot I guess.

This continues until the questioner guesses the correct word. The last person to answer a question before the word is guessed is the next to leave the room and be a questioner.

Other words suitable for Teapot are:

plain (an expanse of flat, level land)
plane (a tool for smoothing wood)

waste (something cast aside as useless)
waist (part of the body)

tee (as in golf)
tea (the beverage)

squall (a storm)
squall (a cry)

bear (the animal)
bare (without clothing)

beet (a vegetable)
beat (to strike)

spar (as in boxing)
spar (mast)

net (a fabric woven or tied with meshes)
net (profit after all expenses are deducted)

pail (a container for liquids)
pale (white- or ashen-looking)

male (a man or boy)
mail (a collection of letters, newspapers, etc.)

see (to look)
sea (the body of water)

pain (feeling of discomfort)
pane (window glass)

tale (a story)
tail (as on a dog or cat)

bored (tired of the whole thing)
board (a piece of lumber)

lean (to rest on for support)
lean (without fat)

lie (to rest as on a bed)
lie (to say something untrue)

gild (to coat with gold)
guild (an association)

Three Matches

You will need: 4 or more players
20 minutes' playing time
3 matches for each player

Each player is provided with three matches. He may put none or as many as he wishes in his right hand. When the host gives the signal all players put their closed right fists out in front. Each player, starting with the host and working around to the left, guesses a number which he feels is *not* the correct total of all the matches being held. A player may guess any number between zero and whatever figure is three times the total number of players.

After each player has made his guess the held matches are shown. Any player who has guessed the correct number is eliminated and the game goes around once more. When only two players are left, the final winner is decided by two out of three guesses.

If four people were playing, 12 would be the highest possible number and the game might go something like this:

Host (who has no matches in his hand) guesses the number 11 as he knows this cannot possibly be correct.

2nd Player (who has three matches in his hand) guesses 5 thinking the total will be more.

3rd Player (who is holding one match) guesses 9.

4th Player (who has one match) guesses 2.

When the hands are opened the matches are totaled and the second player who guessed 5 is eliminated.

Play then goes around again.

4. *Long-playing Games*

HERE's the answer to the one-game evening. Here are games you can play for forty-five minutes or several hours. Whether you plan to play the Race Game or whether it just happens, know that when your guests start one of these games, they'll be around for a long time.

Charades

You will need: 10 to 20 players
1 hour to an evening's playing time
Paper and pencil
An old hat or a cigar box

The guests are divided into two teams. Each team makes a list of the same number of charades as there are members on a team. Charades may be slogans, sayings, people, plays, places, or sometimes words meaning nothing when put together. These are written on separate slips so that the first team may pick one charade at a time from the list made up by the second team.

One member of the first team starts by picking a slip out of a hat and is given three minutes to act out the charade for his teammates. He is not allowed to talk. The other team is the audience. Because they all know what the charade is, the other team finds the guesses and acting amusing. Whether the first team has guessed the right answer or not, its time is up at the end of three minutes. Then a member of the other team picks a slip from the pile made up by the first team and starts acting it out. The timer keeps track of the exact min utes taken for the guessing. The team with the fewest minutes is the winner. The teams alternate back and forth until all the players have had a chance to act out a charade.

There are a number of signals that help your team to understand what you are trying to get across to them. Here are some good starters, but you will probably find that after you have played a few times with the same group, you will originate some of your own.

First, it is important to let your team know what you are going to act out—a book, song title, person, place, etc. You signify a book by holding an imaginary book in your hands and pretending to read. As soon as one of your group calls out "Is it a book?" you nod that it is. Then they try to narrow it down by asking you if it is a classic, a modern novel, an autobiography, a historical novel, etc. If you hear the right classification you point to the person and nod yes again.

The next step is to let the other players know how many words are in the charade by holding up the correct number of fingers. It is wise to choose the key word to act out first, because often when this is guessed you don't have to complete the other words and time is saved.

You can draw a circle on the floor to signify a place, pat the top of your head to let them know you are going to act out a person's name, go into a dance if it is a musical show, draw an imaginary curtain if straight drama. When your team gets warmed up they will follow up immediately with questions to find out if the show is current or old, the person male or female, in this country or not, living or dead, etc.

When you stumble onto a word that seems impossible for you to act out, clench your fists and hit one on top of the other. This means you will act a word that rhymes with the original. When the rhyme is guessed the team suggests words until they hit the one in the charade.

Past tense is indicated by waving over your shoulder. Words such as *and, of, a, the, but, for, in* are shown by holding up your thumb and forefinger about an inch apart. Sometimes it is necessary to break a word down into syllables. This is done by putting up the correct number of fingers for the word, then signifying the number of syllables in this word by showing fingers again. Finally show which syllable you will act out first. You can let one of your teammates know he is getting warm by waving your hands toward yourself. You must do everything with motions; props are not allowed.

To show that you are going to act out the charade all at once, you make big circular motions with your hands. Sometimes it is necessary to signify the cutting of a word by hitting your left hand with the edge of your right palm. You would do this when someone guesses "going" and you just want "go."

The first slip drawn from the hat might be the slogan "It Pays To Use Mollé." Your teammates would call out the different categories. When you hear "slogan" you nod yes. Then you start acting. It's a good thing, if you find yourself on the wrong track, to change your approach and start over again. If they don't seem to be catching on to one word, try another.

Back to "It Pays To Use Mollé." Put up five fingers showing how many words in the charade:

ACTOR: Quickly act out the process of shaving in hopes that someone in the room may guess the right shaving-soap slogan immediately. If not, indicate the first word by holding up one finger and then showing that it's a small one by holding your thumb and forefinger close together. Wait for the group to guess the right small word, nod yes—and on to the second word. Hold up two fingers. Reach into your pocket, place imaginary money on an imaginary counter, and the guesses should start.

GUESS: Money?

ACTOR: Shake head no and continue handing out imaginary money, trying from person to person.

GUESS: Give?

ACTOR: Shake head no but give a stronger "you're getting warm" signal.

GUESS: Pay?

ACTOR: Just the "getting warm" signal.

GUESS: Paid?

ACTOR: More "getting warm" signal.

GUESS: Pays?

ACTOR: Nod yes and on to the third word. Hold up fingers to indicate a short word.

GUESS: In, and, an, a, for, the, to—

ACTOR: Nod yes and signify fourth word by holding up four fingers. Show that you will act out rhyming word by hitting your two fists together. The "rhymer" might be "cues," which you can do by playing imaginary billiards with an imaginary cue stick.

GUESS: Billiards?

ACTOR: Make more use of the imaginary cue stick, aiming at the ball, rubbing chalk on the tip, sliding it through the fingers.

GUESS: Cue?

ACTOR: Give the "getting warm" signal. Indicate several cues.

GUESS: Cues?

ACTOR: Show that the word your teammates are after is part of this by giving the "cutting signal"—the edge of your right hand against your left palm.

GUESS: Use?

ACTOR: On to the fifth word and if they haven't already guessed the slogan, pretend to be shaving again and someone will guess.

GUESS: It Pays To Use Mollé.

Race Charades

You will need: 10 to 20 players
1 hour to an evening's playing time
1 list maker with pencil and paper

This is a variation of regular Charades. The main difference is that the two teams are stationed in different rooms, both acting out the same charades, designated by a list maker who sits midway between the two groups.

The list maker, who can be changed after each group of charades, makes up a list with as many charades as there are members on a team. This means each person will have a chance to get in the act. The list is made up of plays, songs, people, individual words, books, places, magazines, etc. The two teams should be divided by a room or a door, as they will be acting out the same charades and can easily be overheard when the voices get louder and louder. The list maker takes his place halfway between the two teams.

The first member of each team reports to the list maker. They are both given the first charade. They run to their respective rooms and act it out as quickly as possible, using the same signals as in regular Charades. As soon as the charade is guessed correctly, another member runs to the list maker, gives the answer, and gets the next charade. No time should be lost between the correct guess and the next player getting it to the list maker and starting on another.

While one team may take ten minutes to guess some book, the other team may whip through the first three charades only to get stuck on the fourth. As soon as one team completes the list, the game is over and another person makes up a new list.

Paper Charades

You will need: At least 8 players
1 hour to an evening's playing time
Sheets of paper and pencils or two blackboards and chalk

Paper Charades can be varied just as regular Charades with two teams acting out in front of each other in turn, or as Race Charades, with one list maker and two or more teams in different rooms. The big difference is that instead of being acted, the charade is drawn on paper or a blackboard.

This is done by making the same number of horizontal lines on the paper as there are words in the charade. The small words can be shown by shorter lines. The number of syllables in a word can be shown by cutting the horizontal line with the correct number of vertical ones. For example, if the charade to be guessed is ON A BICYCLE BUILT FOR TWO, you indicate the number of words by: ___ ___ _________ _____ ___ ___

The first and second short words would be pointed at, guessed, and filled in. The artist points to the third word and then starts drawing the bicycle. He might skip the fourth word because when the fifth and sixth are guessed that would be guessed quickly.

Another example might be Churchill's *Memoirs,* for which you draw two straight lines and cut the first one into two syllables. After pointing to the first syllable of the first word you draw a church, then point to the second syllable of the first word and draw a hill. To indicate *Memoirs,* you draw a book. No use of actual letters is allowed.

Sight Unseen

You will need: At least 4 couples
About an hour's playing time
Paper and pencils
One object difficult for each couple to draw

This is a drawing game played by couples. One couple at a time is seated in chairs which are back to back. One of them is given a pencil and paper with something to lean on. The other is given an object, such as a lemon, a carving knife, a dust cloth, a fountain pen, an oil can, a pencil sharpener, a baby's rattle, a beer bottle, a box of cereal, a package of cigarettes, a lighter, etc.

The partner with the article in his hand must describe it to his copartner in terms of shape, size, lines, texture. The copartner draws the article as the description goes along, following the descriptions of the invisible object as well as he can.

When the picture is finished, the partners put their names on it. After everyone has had a chance with a different object, all the pictures are put on a table with the objects they are supposed to resemble below them and a vote is taken as to the couple who did the best art work.

Tableau

You will need: At least 10 people
About an hour or more playing time

A tableau is defined as "a representation of an idea by the grouping of persons who remain silent and motionless in appropriate postures." For this less active than Charades game, the guests are divided into three or more teams. Each team makes up its own list of tableaux, which it will demonstrate for the other teams. It is interesting to make the tableaux a little difficult, but if they are so farfetched that none of the other teams can guess within three minutes, there is a point scored *against* the acting team. The Tableau team's score is kept by the minutes it takes the other teams to guess their tableaux.

Number 1 team might have as their first tableau MAN OVERBOARD. This could be shown by one member sitting on the floor yawning in a bored fashion and a man leaning over her. Another example is GIVE ME LIBERTY OR GIVE ME DEATH. The first person in the line could be using the gesture of handing things out; the second one could point to himself; the third one could pose as the Statue of Liberty; the fourth could stand, leaving a little more space between the third team member and himself to denote a connecting word and doing the GIVE gesture; the fifth could point to himself, and the last one could lie stretched out on the floor. If there are fewer members on a team than this, two words may be acted together, such as GIVE ME, with the gesture of pulling your hands toward yourself. Also, you can use the proper names of individual teammates as part of your tableau.

LIST OF TABLEAUX

Love's Labor Lost
Duffy's Tavern
Dear Ruth
Kiss Me Kate (These last three are good if there is a Duffy, Ruth, or Kate in the group)
The Face on the Barroom Floor
Misunderstanding
Pocketful of Rye
Gone with the Wind
Dancing in the Dark
Eat, Drink, and Be Merry
Northwest Passage
Time on My Hands
Two's Company, Three's a Crowd
A Stitch in Time Saves Nine
Look before You Leap

Murder

You will need: At least 8 players
One hour or more playing time
As many slips of paper as there are players

The same number of slips of paper as there are guests are put in a hat. Only on two of the slips is there anything written. On one is *detective* and on the other *murderer*. Everyone present draws a slip of paper from the hat, but no one tells what slip he has.

After all the guests have drawn slips, the lights are turned out in whatever room or rooms the game is to be played in. The detective sits in a chair and doesn't move while the lights are out until the murder has been committed and he is called. All the players move around the room. The murderer stalks his victim and when he thinks the time is right puts his hands around his neck. The victim screams and falls to the floor. Some calm member calls for the detective and he comes to the rescue and asks that the lights be turned on immediately.

He goes to the scene of the crime and all the suspects keep their positions while he makes an investigation. He questions all the players to try to find out who the murderer is. Everyone, with the exception of the murderer, must answer truthfully, but the murderer may answer any way he pleases. The victim must remain silent.

Sometimes the detective is able to discover who the murderer is and sometimes he must give up before the case is solved. Whichever happens, the slips of paper are shuffled and everyone draws from the hat once again.

5. *Fun but Foolish*

STRICTLY nonsense, most of these are good for short-time playing only. But while they last they're fun and you'll probably find one you will want to repeat again and again.

The Orange Game

You will need: 10 to 20 players
About 30 to 45 minutes' playing time
1 orange for each team

This game is only for those who are in a gay mood and willing to look pretty silly. While the aim of passing the orange from one person to another by using only chin and shoulders may sound easy, the execution is difficult.

The first person starts with the orange caught between his chin and shoulder. The next player, using only chin and shoulder, tries to get hold of the orange and in turn pass it on.

It's a cozy affair with great spectator appeal, but if you have more than 10 guests, divide them into two teams racing against each other. The winning team is the first one who relays the orange from the first to the last person in the line.

Even in a race the orange can never be touched with the hands. If it falls to the floor, one of the guilty parties has to get down and pick it up with the same chin-and-shoulder technique.

Poker Face

You will need: At least 8 players
About 20 minutes' playing time
A picture frame about 16 x 20
A watch with a second hand

Each guest in turn takes his place behind the picture frame. The others try to make him laugh or smile by their conversation (no tickling allowed). The time is kept for each person and the one who can hold his poker face the longest is the winner.

Tilly Williams

You will need: At least 6 players
About 20 minutes' playing time

"Tilly Williams is odd and queer but not peculiar." You start the game out of a clear sky. "She likes tennis but not golf, carrots but not beans." And it's up to the rest of the guests to try and figure out why she likes certain things and not others. As each one catches on, he joins the conversation with more of Tilly's likes and dislikes. "She likes apples but not bananas, paddling but not rowing." Sometimes people will think it is the alphabetical placement of the letters, the enunciation of the words. Actually it is just because Tilly Williams is odd and queer, but not peculiar. She likes anything with a double letter in it such as "o*dd*" and "qu*ee*r" and she doesn't like things without double letters such as "peculiar." The game can be continued as long as it is still a mystery to some and they are interested in trying to guess the solution.

Our Cook Doesn't Like Peas

You will need: At least 6 players
About 20 minutes' playing time

This game is a variation of Tilly Williams. Our cook doesn't like peas but she likes beans. She likes cauliflower but she doesn't like green peppers. This time the catch is that our cook doesn't like anything with the letter *P* in it. It isn't necessary to limit the likes and dislikes to vegetables.

My Grandmother

You will need: At least 6 players
About 20 minutes' playing time

This too is a variation of Tilly Williams and there would be no advantage in playing these three games in one evening. If the group caught on to one they would catch on to the others too easily. But they do fill in the lulls in the evening. You might try one with one group and the others with different people.

You start by saying "My grandmother doesn't like tea but she likes coffee. She likes oranges but she doesn't like grapefruit." The guesses will be varied and when one of the other guests guesses the answer he will join in. "My grandmother doesn't like turnips but she likes onions. She likes Fords but she doesn't like Pontiacs." If the guessing comes slowly, you might repeat more often the fact that she doesn't like "tea." The solution is that she doesn't like anything with the letter *T* in it.

Pass the Matchbox

You will need: At least 10 players
About 15 or 20 minutes' playing time
A small wooden matchbox for each team

The guests are divided into two teams and lined up on different sides of the room, so there will be plenty of maneuvering room. The object of the game is for one team to pass the matchbox cover from the first to the last nose without touching it with their hands. A point is counted against the team each time a member touches the matchbox with a hand. The team to get the box from the first to the last person with the fewest number of points against it is the winner.

The Last Straw

You will need: At least 10 players
About 15 or 20 minutes' playing time
A straw for each player
A piece of tissue paper for each team

This is another relay game that is more foolish than skillful but has found its place at many parties. The guests are divided into two teams at different ends of the room. The first person on each team puts the piece of tissue paper (about 3 by 5 inches) on the end of his straw and tries to keep it there by inhaling while he gets it to the next person in line. This player puts his straw on the paper and starts inhaling until it is secure and passes it on to the next one. This continues until the last person on the team has the paper on the end of his straw. The first team to succeed in doing this is the winner.

You may hold the straw with your hands, but you cannot touch the tissue paper. Any person who does has a point counted against his team.

What's a Mugwump?

You will need: At least 10 players
About half an hour's playing time

Either a couple or just one person is sent out of the room while the rest of the guests decide on the definition of some object. They might decide on something like "an old sock" and then each guest is given thirty seconds to make his own definition of an old sock. They must have some answer ready and must use it in answer to all the questions that are asked by the people who went out of the room.

The couple have prepared a list of words while out of the room and when they return begin asking for definitions of these words. All their questions are answered with individual definitions of an "old sock." So the conversation might go like this:

QUESTION: What is my Easter hat?
ANSWER: Something that's been worn too long.
QUESTION: What are Bud's new shoes?
ANSWER: Bud's new shoes are full of holes.
QUESTION: What's Duffy's new car?
ANSWER: Duffy's new car is dirty.
QUESTION: What's my new dress?
ANSWER: Your new dress is something that should be replaced.

And so on until the couple asking for the definitions decides what the unknown article is. The questions can be less personal than the above, but if the individuals in the group are all good friends this might make more laughs. Other words to be defined could be: bubble, kiss, cough, bicycle, tennis racket, automobile, bulldozer, breakfast, etc.

The Ventriloquist

You will need: At least 5 couples
About 20 minutes' playing time

The guests are divided into teams of two each. One person prepares a list of personal questions. He asks the different couples around the room these questions, but the individual to whom they are addressed must wait for her partner to answer. The answer he gives concerns himself.

QUESTION (addressed to young girl): How old are you?

ANSWER (from older partner): Forty next birthday.

QUESTION (addressed to man): What is your great extravagance?

ANSWER (from lady partner): Expensive perfumes.

QUESTION (addressed to girl): What is your waist measurement?

ANSWER (from hefty man): Forty-one inches.

QUESTION (addressed to man): What is your most prized possession?

ANSWER (from dainty girl): My new evening gown.

There's no particular reason for this game except the laughs.

Laughter to Tears

You will need: About 8 or 10 guests
15 minutes' playing time
A coin

The guests sit around the floor in a circle. One member of the party flips a coin in the center of the circle and calls out either "Heads" or "Tails." All the guests are supposed to be expressionless and completely silent. When the coin turns up heads everyone is supposed to laugh, but when the leader picks up the coin they are supposed to wipe the smiles off their faces, stop laughing, and look blank again. When the coin turns up tails, dead silence and blank looks are supposed to continue. Anyone who laughs at the wrong time is out of the game.

Predicament

You will need: At least 8 or 10 players
About a half hour's playing time

One or two players leave the room, depending on the number of guests present. The others decide on some predicament. Each guest makes up his mind what he would do under those circumstances and has this answer ready for the couple when they return to the room. The two out of the room have been thinking up different predicaments to use in their questioning. When they are called back into the room they question the guests to try and discover what predicament has been decided on.

If, for example, the guests left in the room decide on "What would you do if someone in this room asked you for a loan of a thousand dollars?" then each one of them would decide on his individual solution to this problem. The two who have been out of the room would return with a list of emergencies to be used in their questioning. The conversation might go like this:

QUESTION: What would you do if you had unexpected guests?

ANSWER: I'd tell them I was very sorry—but no.

QUESTION: What would you do if your spouse asked you for a divorce?

ANSWER: I'd tell her maybe next year—but not now.

QUESTION: What would you do if your business suddenly failed?

ANSWER: I'd tell them to go jump in the lake.

QUESTION: What would you do if your husband asked you to take a trip to Hawaii?

ANSWER: I'd ask him if he were kidding.

QUESTION: What would you do if your dog bit you?

ANSWER: I'd tell him to go pick on Ed.

When the predicament has been guessed, two more people go out of the room and another emergency is decided upon.

My Bequest

You will need: At least 10 players
About half an hour's playing time
A slip of white paper and a slip of colored paper for each guest

Each guest is given a slip of white paper on which he writes some disliked possession and a piece of colored paper on which he writes his reason for giving it up.

All the bequests are put in one hat and all the reasons for giving them up in another. Each guest steps up and pulls a bequest out of the first hat and reads it aloud, then out of the next hat takes a piece of colored paper on which is written the reason for giving it up. As they have all been well shuffled, the two no longer go together. Here are a few examples of what can happen in the shuffle:

BEQUESTS	REASONS FOR GIVING UP
My double chin	It won't curl
My bald head	Makes it hard to breathe
My long feet	Want to start all over again
My bad disposition	Makes my eyelids swell
My age	Makes me poor
My big nose	Makes me mad
My asthma	Nobody likes me
My mother-in-law	Can't button my collar
My straight hair	Makes me cross-eyed
My allergies	Can't find shoes to fit them
My income taxes	Makes me look old

Your Favorite Object

You will need: About 8 or 10 guests
20 minutes' playing time

Each guest is told to decide on some favorite object and to answer when he is questioned with his object in mind. The host goes around the room asking several people what their favorite objects are, until he finds one that he wants to be used as the subject for the questions. If perfume were the object decided on, the host would start thus:

QUESTION: When do you use perfume?

ANSWER (with his car in mind): I use perfume when I go out.

QUESTION: Why do you use perfume?

ANSWER (with hair oil in mind): I use perfume because it's good for my scalp.

QUESTION: How do you use perfume?

ANSWER (thinking of his golf clubs): When I use perfume, I swing as hard as I can.

QUESTION: How often do you use perfume?

ANSWER (thinking of her new dress): I haven't had a chance to use perfume yet.

Going to Europe

You will need: At least 8 players
About 20 minutes' playing time

"I'm sailing for Europe next week and I'm taking with me some handkerchiefs," the first guest might say. The catch is that he is going to take to Europe something that begins with his first initial. The next person, whose name is Marion, says "I'm sailing for Europe next week and I'm going to take some money" The next person tries to understand what the trick is. If he guesses wrong, he is told he can't go to Europe yet. The game continues until everyone catches on.

Pinchy Winchy

You will need: At least 8 or 10 players
About 10 minutes' playing time
A burned cork

One person is appointed the victim without his knowledge. The guests stand around in a circle, with the host to the left of the victim. The host starts by telling the victim to do whatever he does to the guest next to him. He pinches the victim's cheek. The victim turns to the person on his right and does and says the same thing, and so it goes around the circle. When it gets back to the host, he turns to the victim and says "Pinchy winchy" and pinches him on the other cheek. This continues around the circle again. What is actually happening is that the victim is being all marked up with burned cork. If the laughs don't give it away, he may spend a great part of the evening walking around marked up.

The host can be fooled too. If the person on his left pretends nothing is happening, he can very easily slip some of the black cork on his fingers and give the host the same treatment the victim is getting.

Signature

You will need: Any number of players
About 10 or 15 minutes' playing time
Paper and pencil

The host puts a sheet of paper on the wall and then the contest starts. The problem is to write your name on the sheet with your right hand (if you are right-handed) and swing your left leg clockwise in a circle. It's just a simple trick in co-ordination, but watch the effort that goes into it.

6. *There's a Trick to It*

SIMPLE fill-in games, these tricks are done by one or two people with the rest of the group guessing the solution. Start one and you'll have a hard time working in the second: you'll find that most of your guests have a favorite of their own they are anxious to try.

Cahoots

You will need: At least 8 players
About half an hour's playing time

Cahoots takes two people who know the "trick." The collaborator may close his eyes, go into the next room, or turn his back to the group, just as long as he doesn't see what's going on. The game starts with one of the partners pointing to different people in the room and asking "Do you point as I point?" He can ask this five or ten times and then asks, "Are you in cahoots?" The collaborator says yes or no. If he says yes the pointer then asks, "At whom am I pointing?" The collaborator gives him the correct name.

This is the trick: the first pointing with the question "Do you point as I point?" is just done at random. But when the pointer asks, "Are you in cahoots?" the collaborator knows that the last person to have spoken or laughed is the person at whom the partner will point when he asks "At whom am I pointing?" If there is any confusion in the room, so that the collaborator is not sure of the last person to have identified himself by a sound, he will answer no when asked "Are you in cahoots?" and they will start over again.

This or That?

You will need: At least 8 or 10 players
About 20 minutes' playing time

This is another trick that two people must be in on. Four guests are placed in a row and after the "guesser" goes out of the room, one of these people is chosen as IT. When the guesser comes back into the room, he tells the group which person has been chosen by answering yes when his partner asks "Is it this one, is it that one?" etc.

The trick is that each person has been labeled THIS or THAT in order. For instance, the man on the left is THIS, the person next him is THAT, the next one THIS, the last one on the right THAT. When the pointer asks, "Is it this one?" or "Is it that one?" he uses the label that was secretly given to them EXCEPT when he is pointing to the designated person, then he calls THIS THAT or vice versa, to give his collaborator the signal. When the pointer uses the wrong adjective then his partner knows he is pointing to the right guest.

Good Guess

You will need: At least 8 players
About 20 minutes' playing time
A large sheet of paper or a blackboard

This game is one of the many variations of This or That? You need two people who know the secret. Draw three columns of crosses on the paper or blackboard. After one of the partners goes out of the room, one cross is designated and the partner comes back in. His problem is to guess which cross has been picked and of course he does.

The trick is to label the two outside rows of crosses THIS and the inside one THAT. The right adjective is used in asking "Is it this?" or "Is it that?" until the partner wants to let his collaborator know which cross has been chosen. Then he points to a cross in one of the outside rows and calls it "That," or one in the inside row and calls it "This."

Five in a Row

You will need: At least 8 players
About 15 or 20 minutes' playing time
5 objects, such as books, magazines, etc.

Five objects which can be numbered 1, 2, 3, 4, 5, such as fingers held up, books on the floor, or five pieces of paper on the wall, are used for this game. This one also takes two people who know the trick. One of the two goes out of the room and the group picks out one of the five objects for the collaborator to guess. When he returns to the room his partner points to the different objects asking, "Is it this one?" If on the third question he points to the third object, his collaborator will know that that's the one.

Here's the trick: the objects are secretly numbered from left to right, 1, 2, 3, 4, 5. When the number of the question and the number of the object are the same, then the collaborator knows that's IT.

Nine Books

You will need: At least 8 players
About 20 minutes' playing time
9 books and a cane or umbrella to use as a pointer

This is another game for two people to understand and the rest of the group to guess. Nine books are placed on the floor in rows of threes. One of the two guests leaves the room. While he is out the group selects one of the books for him to identify as IT.

When the collaborator returns to the room, his partner points to the different books, asking "Is it this one?" "Is it this one?" "Is it that one?" etc. When he points to the spot on a book that is similar to its position on the floor the partner knows that's IT. For instance, if the book in the lower left-hand corner has been designated, the pointer would point to the lower left-hand corner of the book that's in that position on the floor. The aid will answer yes when asked, "Is it this one?"

As each of the guests thinks he knows the solution, he can go out of the room and take a stab at it.

Who's the Owner?

You will need: At least 8 players
About 20 minutes' playing time

A "mind reader" and a confederate work together on this trick and claim that without being told the mind reader can guess who owns a designated object. The mind reader leaves the room and his partner is given something that belongs to one of the guests. He takes the article in his hand and calling the mind reader to return to the room asks, "Who's the owner?" The mind reader looks at his confederate and then starts concentrating and guesses the correct owner.

The trick is for the partner holding the object to take the same position as the owner of this object. The mind reader while concentrating can check the different positions around the room and then determine who the owner is.

Crossed or Uncrossed

You will need: About 8 players
About 15 minutes' playing time
A pair of scissors

One person starts the game by passing a pair of scissors around the circle of guests and saying "I received these scissors uncrossed and I pass them to you crossed." The next person tries to guess what the catch is and is told whether he is right or not.

The trick is in the position of the feet or legs when the scissors are received. If the feet are uncrossed, the guest receives the scissors uncrossed. To confuse the next person he might cross his feet before passing the scissors on to him and say "And I pass them crossed."

It is also confusing to the person who doesn't know the trick if you open and close the scissors as you receive and pass them. They often think that this has something to do with whether they are "crossed or uncrossed."

Automobile Show

You will need: About 8 players
About 15 minutes' playing time

The two people who know this trick are the salesman and his customer. The customer leaves the room and the others decide on the name of a car. When the customer returns, the salesman will name different cars and the customer will be able to tell him when he mentions the one chosen by the group.

The signal on this is for the salesman to show by the number of fingers on his lap whether it will be the first car mentioned or the tenth. He shows two fingers if it is the second car mentioned, three for the third car, etc.

The Berries

You will need: At least 8 players
About 20 minutes' playing time

Two of the guests get the others guessing what the trick is to this one. An aid is sent from the room while the rest decide on an object or a place for him to identify. When he is called back, his partner asks him questions such as "Is it Pike's Peak?" "Is it mashed potatoes?" "Is it the New York Central Railroad?" "Is it a baked apple?" "Is it strawberries?" "Is it a book?" To this last question the aid would answer yes.

The clue to this is that it is always the place or object mentioned after the small fruit. The signal word can be changed from strawberry to cherry, raspberry, blackberry, currant, loganberry, gooseberry, snowberry, grape, etc.

Radar

You will need: At least 8 players
About 20 minutes' playing time
Pencil and paper

In this game there is a mind reader and his confederate, but the confederate is not known to the group. The mind reader tells the guests that he has the power to read from a folded paper with his eyes closed. Each of the guests writes a short sentence on a slip of paper, folds the paper, and hands it to him. After all the guests have written a sentence and passed them to the mind reader, he picks out one, presses it against his forehead, closes his eyes, and reads "Now is the time." Without unfolding the paper, he asks, "Who wrote that?" and his confederate acknowledges that this is his statement.

The mind reader then unfolds the piece of paper and continues the trick quickly before there is a demand from any of the guests to look at the paper. He remembers what was written on the first piece of paper and when he presses the paper to his forehead this time is able to quote a sentence actually written by one of the guests. The catch to this is for the confederate to admit to any sentence the mind reader mentions first, so that when he looks at the first slip of paper, he is able to memorize an actual sentence that has been written by one of the guests. In this way he can keep one jump ahead on the sentences. To prevent a slip-up, the confederate should make a pencil mark on the outside of his own folded slip so that the mind reader won't use that sentence.

What's the City?

You will need: At least 8 players
About 15 or 20 minutes' playing time

A mind reader and his assistant work on this trick together. While the mind reader is out of the room, the guests decide on the name of a city. When he returns, the assistant names different cities and the mind reader knows when the right city has been named.

The clue is to name a city with two words before the right one. Some of the clue cities could be: New York, New Orleans, Buenos Aires, San Jose, San Francisco, Kansas City, Los Angeles, Mexico City, Oklahoma City, St. Louis, New Haven, St. Paul, San Antonio, Jersey City, Fort Worth, San Diego, Grand Rapids, Long Beach, Des Moines, El Paso, Corpus Christi, South Bend, Fall River, New Bedford, Newport News, Palo Alto, Santa Barbara, Panama City, etc.

He Can Do Little

You will need: At least 8 players
About 10 minutes' playing time
A cane, yardstick, or umbrella

The trickster uses a pointer and draws a picture on the floor, saying as she draws, "I am drawing a picture of a man; he can do little who can't do this." To confuse the guests she might stand in a funny position, and in imitating her they will think that this is the answer. The real trick in imitating the leader is to realize that she is doing this with her left hand. Most of the imitators will not notice this and will pick up the pointer with their right hands.

The Magic Touch

You will need: At least 8 players
About 15 or 20 minutes' playing time
Three articles

Two of the players must be "in the know" for this game and understand the signals. The first confederate goes out of the room and the other asks that someone touch any one of three articles that are on a table. The other player is called back into the room. He makes a few mysterious gestures over the articles and then guesses which one was touched.

The secret behind this is in the words used to call the player back into the room. If the first article has been touched the player left in the room would call the other one back with "All right." If it is the second article, he will say, "Come back." If the third, "Ready." These can be easily remembered by their position in the alphabet. The articles should be mentally numbered reading from left to right as the guesser sees them.

If they want to make the signals more confusing, they can decide that article No. 1 is any consonant up to *L,* article No. 2 is any vowel, and article No. 3 is any consonant from *M* to the end of the alphabet.

That's It

You will need: At least 8 players
About 15 or 20 minutes' playing time

One of the two confederates goes out of the room and the rest of the group decide on one object which the guesser will be able to identify when he returns. The confederate who has stayed in the room calls the other back and tells him that he will touch various articles in the room, one of which has been selected for him to identify. When he touches the chosen article, he is to let him know. After he walks around the room touching different articles, he finally points to the one that has been selected and asks, "Is this it?" and the confederate answers, "That's it."

The trick is to touch something black just before you touch the object to be identified. You could change the signal to something red, something white, something with legs.

From One to Fifty

You will need: At least 8 players
About 20 minutes' playing time

While one of the confederates is out of the room, the guests decide on any even number under 50—for instance, it might be 16. When he returns the questioner, who knows the signals, asks, "Is it 40?" This question tells the one who has been out of the room that he should listen for another clue in the fourth question. The questioner asks a second and third question, which are just fillers. Then he will ask, "Is it 28?" That will tell the aid to multiply 2 x 8 for the correct answer. When he is asked, "Is it 16," he will already have the answer.

It is best to change the clue question, sometimes asking for 30, 22, or 50. The first number in the opening question always tells what question to watch for to multiply for the final answer.

Pick a Number

You will need: At least 8 players
About 20 minutes' playing time

This is a variation of From One to Fifty. The method is more direct. After the aid has left the room, the guests may choose any number. The clue is in the first question, which might be "Is it 52?" This means you add these two numbers together and know that the correct answer will be the seventh question.

The Sticky Dime

You will need: Any number of players
About 10 minutes' playing time
A dime

One person who isn't acquainted with the trick is chosen to be the victim. You explain to him that you are going to place a dime on his forehead. It has no glue on it, but it will stick. His challenge is to shake it off in one minute.

Then you press the dime hard against his forehead and take it off. He will think that the dime is still there. Before his time is up, drop the dime on the floor as though he has shaken it off himself. This might work once or twice with the same person. Of course, he is told to keep his hand away from his forehead.

The Circle

You will need: At least 8 players
About 20 minutes' playing time

The guests sit in a circle and the two confederates sit and study the group thoughtfully. One of the confederates leaves the room and the guests change their positions. When he returns he turns his back to the group, but is able to tell immediately at whom his confederate is pointing.

The trick is to notice the fourth person from the pointer's left before the positions are changed. When the guesser returns to the room, the pointer always indicates the person who was fourth from his left before the positions were changed.

Three of a Kind

You will need: At least 8 players
About 15 minutes' playing time
3 similar objects

The three objects could be three magazines, windowpanes, books, etc. While the confederate has his back turned, or goes out of the room, the object for him to identify is chosen. He picks it immediately, saying, "It's the middle one." Or, "It's the one on the right."

His confederate has given him the clue by putting his finger to his mouth, either to the center or the right or left side. If he has a pencil in his hand, he may use this.

Another clue for this could be the placement of the hands. If it is the center object he could hold his hands far apart, the left hand over the right one would indicate the object on the left, or the right hand over the left would indicate the object on the right.

What Time Is It?

You will need: At least 8 players
About 15 minutes' playing time

While one of the confederates is out of the room a certain hour is decided on. When he returns to the room, he listens to the host's remark and is able to guess the hour.

If four o'clock were the chosen hour, the host might say to his confederate, "Don't worry, you'll get it." The guesser would know from the first letter in the first word that he should guess four o'clock, because this is the fourth letter in the alphabet.

Psychic

You will need: At least 8 players
About 15 minutes' playing time

This trick can be done with the knowledge of only one or two people. The group talks up the possibility of certain people having psychic powers without realizing it. As proof of this, one or two are sent from the room after having been told that it is possible to communicate a thought from one person to another.

The group left in the room is supposed to pick out an object in plain sight and concentrate on it so that this thought will be sent to the one or two people who have left the room. When the victim guesses something the first time, right away the other guests say, as though amazed, "That's it!" The trick is for them to say yes to anything the victim guesses the first time.

Sometimes the victim thinks there may be thought waves slipping through the air and sometimes a more skeptical victim will think it's just coincidence. So it's best to try again. This time, it might be wise to make it the second guess.

Concentrate

You will need: At least 8 players
About 10 minutes' playing time
Pencil and paper

One of the guests suggests that he go out of the room while the group decides on four words to be written on a slip of paper. If they will concentrate on these words, he claims he will be able to write the same thing. The other guests cooperate and write four words on a piece of paper. The magician returns to the room, writes "the same thing" on his slip of paper, and hands it to one of the guests who has remained in the room, asking him to read it out loud. He opens the paper and reads *The same thing.*

The Fingerprint

You will need: About 8 or 10 players
About 10 minutes' playing time
A tumbler and a coin

This game takes a concealed confederate who gives a signal.

One of the guests claims that he can place a glass upside down on a table, place a coin on top of the glass, and then be able to tell who has taken the coin after he leaves the room.

When he returns to the room he requests that each person place his first finger on the glass, one at a time. Then he picks up the glass, holds it to his ear, and tells who has the coin.

The secret is to have the confederate place his finger on the glass immediately after the person who has the coin.

The Barnyard

You will need: At least 8 or 10 players
About 5 minutes' playing time

This one is short and silly. One of the guests goes around the room giving to each one the name of an animal he is supposed to imitate. Instead of actually doing this, he tells all but one to keep silent and this guest he instructs to crow like a rooster. When he gives the command of one, two, three—there is complete silence except for the loud crowing of one guest.

Copy Cat

You will need: About 8 or 10 players
About 15 minutes' playing time

One of the guests claims that no one in the room can say the same sentence he does in the same way. Using "I'm having a wonderful time" and changing the inflection of his voice each time, he goes around the group letting each person imitate him, one at a time. The trick is to clear the voice before the sentence each time.

Match Jump

You will need: Any number of players
Playing time until trick is solved
10 matches

This one can take any length of time. If your guests are the patient type they will probably insist on trying to solve this themselves. Sometimes they give up and ask for the answer.

You place 10 matches in a row and ask someone to try to cross all the matches by jumping over only two at a time. Matches already crossed count as two.

It's advisable to have extra matches available so that different groups can try their hand at it.

This is how it is done: take the fifth match from the left, jump it over two to the left, and cross the match next to the end; take the fourth match from the right, jump two matches to the right, and cross the end match; then the second uncrossed match on the left jumps two matches to the right; the uncrossed match on the left end jumps the two crossed matches toward the center; and the uncrossed one in the middle jumps two crossed ones on the right.

Nine to Ten

You will need: Any number of players
Unlimited playing time
9 matches

This one is good for the trick repertoire, as it is easy to remember. The host places 9 matches on a table and asks the guests to make 10 out of them. You spell out the word TEN with the 9 matches.

Match Squares

You will need: Any number of players
Unlimited playing time
About 15 matches

Five squares are formed with matches, three squares adjoining one another in one row, another square on top of

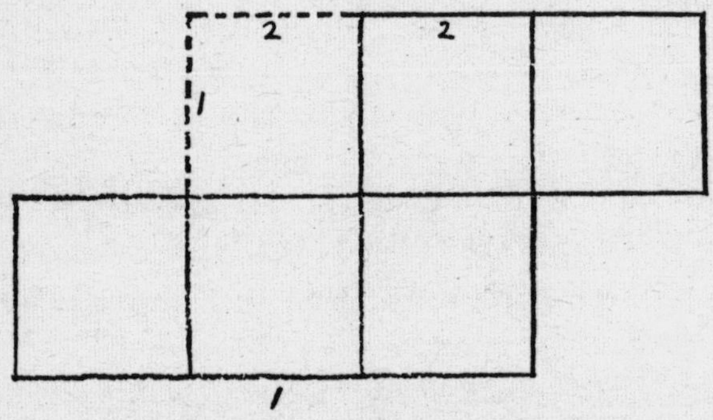

the square on the right, and the fifth one adjoining the last. You are asked to move two matches to make four squares. See diagram for solution.

Match Triangles

You will need: Any number of players
Unlimited playing time
6 matches

Place the six matches so that two triangles are formed with one point of each touching. The problem is to move three matches to make four triangles. This is done by moving the three matches in the bottom triangle so that they are in an upright position over the other triangle and form three triangles. Each match is placed at the three angles and held in pyramid fashion over the flat triangle.

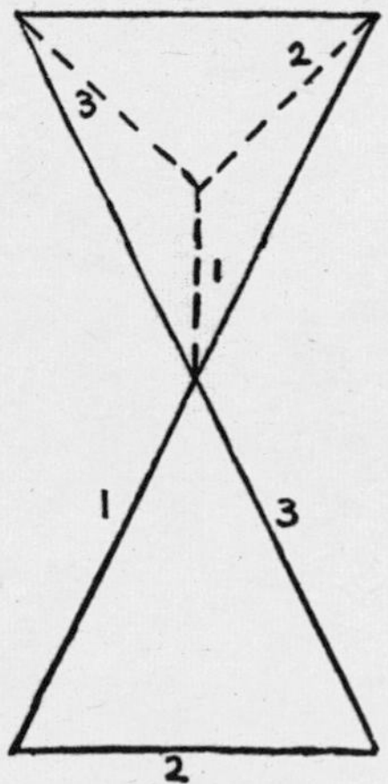

Five Glasses

You will need: Any number of players
Unlimited playing time
5 Old-fashioned glasses

Five Old-fashioned glasses are placed on a table. The problem is to arrange them so that they all touch one another. This one is tough.

To accomplish this feat, two of the glasses are placed on their sides, one inside the other. A third glass is placed on the left on its side and a fourth on the right on its side, with the fifth one upside down covering all of them.

The Jigger Trick

You will need: Any number of players
About 15 minutes' playing time
2 jiggers, one full of water, one full of whisky
A thin piece of cardboard, something like a business card

This is a spectator trick and a fascinating one. The jigger of whisky is placed on a table. The jigger of water is filled to the brim, covered with the thin piece of cardboard, and placed upside down over the jigger of whisky. Very carefully the cardboard is pulled away from one side of the two jiggers, so that a very small hole, not much bigger than a pinhead, allows the trick to begin.

Then you sit back and watch it happen. Drop by drop the water falls into the jigger of whisky and forces the whisky drop by drop into the top glass. When the trick is completed, the jigger on the bottom is full of water and the jigger on the top is full of whisky.

Five Coins

You will need: Any number of players
Unlimited playing time
3 dimes and 2 pennies

The five coins are put on a table in a row of a dime, a penny, a dime, a penny, a dime. The trick is to figure out how all the dimes can be put on one side and all the pennies on the other by moving two coins at a time in three moves. The coins you move must be alongside each other and must be moved in this order. It's this easy when you know how. Numbering the coins from 1 to 5 from the left, move 3 and 4 to the left end, move 2 and 3 into the space on the right, and 4 and 5 into the space on the left.

Nine Squares

You will need: Any number of players
15 minutes' playing time
Pencil with eraser and paper for each guest

This is good for one time playing only, but until you learn the secret combination of numbers, it is quite a puzzler.

Guests draw a square and then divide it into 9 small boxes by drawing 2 horizontal and 2 vertical lines. Each number from 1 through 9 is to be placed in the boxes, so that whether you add them horizontally, vertically, or diagonally the answer is 15. Each number may be used only once.

The solution is worked out by placing the numbers so that reading from left to right you have: first line—2, 9, 4; second line—7, 5, 3; third line—6, 1, 8.

Where's the Nickel?

You will need: Any number of players
About 10 or 15 minutes' playing time
Any two coins

The host puts two coins on the table, for instance, a nickel and a penny. He turns his back and asks one of the guests to put one hand on his head and the other on his stomach. He asks him to put the hand that's on his head over the nickel and the other one over the penny. He then tells him he will be able to guess where the nickel is. The host turns around, looks at the guest's hands, and points to the one over the nickel.

The trick to this is to keep the hand on the head long enough so that you can tell the difference in the color between the two hands. The one that's been on the head is much paler because some of the blood has drained out of it while it's been in that position. The host will probably be asked to repeat this several times while people guess the solution. He can switch the guessing around and say he can guess which hand is over the penny.

Odd or Even?

You will need: Any number of players
About 10 or 15 minutes' playing time
5 or 10 one-dollar bills

The host asks one of the guests to fold a dollar bill in quarters, with Washington's face on the outside. The guest then shows him that quarter of the folded bill which bears the signature of the Secretary of the Treasury. The host claims that from looking at that signature he can guess whether the bill serial number in the upper right-hand corner is an odd or even number.

The trick is that just above the Secretary's signature is a letter of the alphabet. If the letter is A, the number will be odd; B, even; C, odd; D, even and so on through the alphabet.

7. *Thirty-two Different Varieties*

As THE VARIETY which is the spice of any party these are the games which can be served to your guests in any combination and still make good playing. There's a type for everyone.

Test Kitchen

You will need: 8 or more players
Half hour's playing time
Pencil and paper for each guest
10 liquids such as coffee, tea, orange juice, lemon juice, grapefruit juice, water, milk, cider, etc.

Even people with a sharp sense of taste become confused

when trying one thing after another, particularly if they cannot see the color. Because color is so important in this you may either blindfold each guest as he taste-tests or add a few drops of vegetable coloring to each liquid. This will change the liquid's appearance, but not the taste.

The guests have slips numbered for each liquid and they try to identify each by taste alone. The one who guesses the greatest number correctly is the winner.

Alphabet Rhythm

You will need: 10 to 20 players
15 minutes' to one hour's playing time

A mildly active game, this is kind to anyone in a room beneath because guests stay seated throughout. Let them sit where they are, on chairs, on the floor, even on the staircase, but it's easiest if you can develop something resembling a circle, or enough of a line of succession so that a player always knows when it's his turn.

The game is played to a rhythm similar to the *one, two, three–kick* of the Conga and is executed by everyone–in unison–clapping his hands on his knees for three beats and then snapping his fingers in the air for the fourth.

Get the rhythm started and then on the fourth beat say some letter of the alphabet such as J. The player on your right must answer with a word beginning with J and then on the next fourth beat say another letter of the alphabet. And so on around the room.

All letters and all words may be said only on the fourth beat. The game continues around to the right until someone makes a mistake by speaking off beat, hesitating with a word or letter, repeating the letter which was given to him, or failing to answer in his turn.

Each person is allowed three mistakes before he drops from

the game. The speed of the rhythm helps determine the difficulty of the game. If you want to make it really tough, up the beat to a fast pace and make it a rule that no word can be repeated.

Up Jenkins

You will need: 8 or more players
15 minutes' playing time

This game can be played at a dining-room table, at a long coffee table, or with the guests seated on the floor. The players are divided into two teams and face each other on the floor or across the table.

One team is given a dime, which they pass up and down the line under the table, or behind their backs if they are seated on the floor. Any one of their opponents may at any time say "Up, Jenkins," which means all members of the team with the dime must place their hands in fists on the table or on the floor. At "Down, Jenkins," they must open their fists and place their hands palms down.

The opposing team must now try to decide which palm covers the dime. When they point to a player's hand and say "Down, Jenkins," that player must remove his hand. This proceeds until they find the dime, which is then given to the other team to hide.

Naturally, all players on the team with the dime try to do the same thing: either each pretends he is the one with the dime or each pretends he doesn't have it.

Score is kept by counting one point for every palm which is removed before the dime is discovered. The team with the lowest score wins.

Fifty-six

You will need: 10 to 16 players
30 minutes to one hour's playing time

This is a sit-down game. The amount of concentration it requires depends upon a player's natural ability with multiplication tables, and whether or not he can think about a number and clap his hands at the same time.

Using 7 as the number which can never be said aloud, the guests start counting off from 1 to 56, going clockwise around the room. When the counting reaches any number which includes a 7 or is a multiple of 7, that player must clap his hands instead of saying the number. After each clap the counting reverses and runs counter-clockwise.

So it goes 1-2-3-4-5-6-clap. Counter-clockwise 8-9-10-11-12-13-clap. Clockwise 15-16-clap. Counter-clockwise 18-19-etc. Twenty-seven-28 is a difficult combination because it requires a double clap and a double reverse.

The counting should go rapidly. Taking too much time, speaking or clapping out of turn, or saying a wrong number is a mistake. When this happens the person making the mistake starts the game again at any number between 1 and 7.

Players may either be dropped after three mistakes or may throw a chip into the pot for each mistake. The pot then goes to the person who finally says 56.

If the game proves popular, vary it by changing the unspoken number to 8 and count to 64, or 9 and count to 81.

Stick Pin

You will need: 8 or more players
10 minutes' playing time
Several packages of common pins
A small bowl

Replacing common pins in their original paper takes more time than most people would imagine, and when grouped with other simple tests of skill can provide an entire evening's entertainment.

Remove all the pins from the paper and place them in a bowl. The paper is then cut into strips (there should be at least two strips for every guest).

The bowl of pins is placed in the center of the room and at a signal players start replacing pins in their proper holes. If you have up to 13 guests, have them play individually. For more than this, teams of two are better than single competition.

Ping Pong Basketball

You will need: 8 or more players
15 minutes' playing time
A No. 10 tin can with one end removed
5 ping pong balls

An empty No. 10 tin can becomes the basket for this game. Place the can on the floor and with a book, ruler, or magazine indicate a distance of 10 feet. Players must stand anywhere in back of this line and attempt to throw the 5 ping pong balls into the can. They score one point for each ball dropped into the can.

Sew a Button

You will need: 8 or more players
10 minutes' playing time
At least 10 buttons of assorted sizes for each guest
An 8-inch-square scrap of material for each guest
Needle and thread for each guest

This game can be limited to male players alone, or can be played with teams of one man and one girl.

Put all the buttons in a dish and provide each player with a needle and a spool or a length of thread. At a signal, guests thread their needles and race to see who can sew on the most buttons in the given time. The buttons may be sewn with one continuous thread or, to make it more difficult, you can say the thread must be broken with each button. The winner is the individual with the most buttons, or the team with highest total between them.

Card Flip

You will need: 2 or more players
15 minutes' playing time
A deck of old playing cards
A man's hat

The hat is placed on the floor about 5 feet from the player's chair. The object is to flip as many cards as possible into the hat. This can be done in whatever manner the player chooses as long as he doesn't lean over the line. One point is scored for each card that lands in the hat and each person counts his score as he finishes.

If you have a large number of guests score them by teams. For smaller groups, individual scoring is better.

Take a Base

You will need: 10 or more players
At least half an hour's playing time
4 books or magazines

A baseball diamond is laid out on the floor by placing books or magazines as first base, second base, third base, and home plate.

The group is divided into two teams of players and the host announces that he will be pitcher and umpire for both teams. The first member of the team at bat takes his place at home plate and is asked a true-or-false question by the host. If the player's answer is correct, it counts as a base hit and he goes to first, with another player replacing him at home plate. If he misses a question it counts as an out. Three outs retire the team and the second team comes to bat. A run is scored only if 4 questions have been answered correctly.

One team may make up the questions for the opposing side, or the true-and-false questions found on page 94 may be used. If this game proves popular with your guests, you might try such variations as grading questions as 1, 2, or 3 bag hits with a home run the award for the most difficult questions. In this case each team elects a pitcher, who then decides what questions he will try on members of the opposition.

Words and Pictures

You will need: 8 or more guests
Half an hour's playing time
A copy of an old magazine for each couple
Several copies of old newspapers
Several pairs of scissors
Scotch tape or glue

Divide the guests into teams of two each and give each team a copy of an old magazine. The teams are to select two pictures and then, using newspapers as source material, clip words, sentences, or paragraphs which will form stories for their pictures. No written words can be used to fill in; everything must come from a newspaper. When all the stories are pasted together and attached to the pictures, they are collected for judgment according to their value as a news story and completeness.

Cootie

You will need: 4 or more players
Half an hour's playing time
Paper and pencil for each guest
Dice

This game is best when played with groups of four or five. If you have a large number of guests, divide them into smaller units so that a player will not have too long a wait for his turn.

Each player marks his paper into 8 squares and in the first square draws that legendary animal the cootie. The cootie has six parts, one for each number on dice. They are:

Number 1	A body	*Number 4*	Eyes
Number 2	A head	*Number 5*	A tail
Number 3	Legs	*Number 6*	Feelers on his head

The guest lists and numbers each of the six parts on his paper and then sets about filling in his squares with each part in just that order.

Players shake the dice in turn, with only one shake allowed each time. As the squares must be filled in order, guests attempt to roll a 1. Failing to do so, they must wait their turn to try again. Once a guest has filled in square 1, or the cootie's body, he then rolls for a 2, or the cootie's head.

Play for everyone stops when the first guest completes a cootie. He gets a bonus of 5 points and everyone else scores one point for each filled-in box.

Groups may remain as they were, or high and low scores in each group change places before play is resumed. High scorer for all games wins.

Quiz Program

You will need: 10 or more players
Half an hour's playing time
A set of questions and answers
A watch with a second hand

Guests are divided into two teams and each group selects its own captain. The host asks the team to his right the first question, allowing 30 seconds for an answer. While the team members may contribute their suggestions and talk over the answer among themselves, it is only the captain who gives the final answer to the host.

When a team cannot answer a question with one try, the same question is put to the second team. If the second team can answer the question, it gets a point for answering the opposing team's question. If the second team cannot answer it, no one scores, for a score is made only when a team correctly answers a question on which its opponents failed.

The host may prepare his own list of questions before the party, or the following true-or-false questions may be used for Quiz Program.

True and False Questions

1. In a calendar year, spring wheat is harvested before winter wheat.

   False: Winter wheat is harvested in the spring, while spring wheat is harvested in late summer or early fall.

2. The ginger we eat is extracted from the leaf of the ginger plant.

   False: The ginger which we eat is the rootstock (underground stem) of the plant.

3. The subsoil is the best soil for growing large crops.

   False: It's the layer beneath the topsoil and is not well suited to growing crops.

4. Many bats used by the major leagues are more than thirty-six inches long.

   True: They can be as long as forty-two inches.

5. To see the source of the Mississippi River you would have to go to Canada.

   False: Minnesota.

6. A cube has six sides.
   True
7. The Petrified Forest is in Arizona.
   True
8. The king on our present day playing cards is reputed to be Henry the Eighth.
   True
9. Sir Joshua Reynolds was primarily a landscape painter.
   False: He was one of the greatest of English portrait painters.
10. Morro Castle is at the entrance of Havana Harbor.
    True
11. Thomas Mann was a noted reformer in the field of American education.
    False: Horace Mann was the educator.
12. The following lines are quoted correctly: "A tisket, a tasket, a red and yellow basket."
    False: That famous basket was green and yellow.
13. All plants are green.
    False: Indian pipes, puffballs, mushrooms, and many others are not.
14. Escrow is a bitter green salad.
    False: It's a sealed instrument of law.
15. In area South America is larger than North America.
    False: North America–8,000,000 square miles
    South America–7,000,000 square miles
16. When the mouse in the nursery rhyme ran up the clock, the clock struck twelve.
    False: It struck one.
17. Jane Austen and Jane Eyre were both English novelists.
    False: *Jane Eyre* is a book by Charlotte Brontë.
18. Chicago is the geographic center of the United States.
    False: The geographic center is in Kansas.

19. Reno, Nevada is farther west than Los Angeles, California.

True: By about one hundred miles

20. When a ship docks at Los Angeles it passes through the Golden Gate.

False: San Francisco has the Golden Gate at her entrance.

21. A lumberjack is a device for hoisting great logs onto flat cars.

False: A lumberjack is a man.

22. In checkers, when there is no handicap, each player starts off with 12 men.

True

23. Alaska is part of continental United States.

False: Continental United States means the forty-eight states, bounded by Canada, Mexico, the Atlantic, and the Pacific.

24. 1849 was the year of the great gold rush to Alaska.

False: 1899 was the year of the Alaskan Gold Rush. 1849 was the year of the California Gold Rush.

25. Wheat is often stored in elevators.

True: They are great shafts in which wheat is stored.

26. The famous Kimberley Diamond Mines are in Africa.

True: They are in South Africa.

27. All newspapers use the same kind of type.

False: Those in common use are Bodoni, Caslon, Cheltenham, Gothic, etc.

28. United States mail has been carried by rail for more than one hundred years.

True: It was first carried by the South Carolina Railroad in November, 1831.

29. There is a United States mint in Denver.

True: Denver, San Francisco, and Philadelphia have United States mints.

30. The President's signature appears on all current paper currency.

False: Only those of the Secretary of the Treasury and the Treasurer

31. The Sleepy Hollow made famous by Washington Irving is in New York State.

True: Near Tarrytown

32. The Spanish Main was in the Pacific Ocean.

False: It is the name formerly given to the southern part of the Caribbean.

33. The Kentucky Derby is usually held at Churchill Downs.

True: In Louisville, Kentucky

34. Finnan haddie is made of fish.

True: It's smoked haddock.

35. The acoustic of a plane corresponds to the steering wheel of an automobile.

False: Acoustic has to do with sound waves.

36. The Lincoln Memorial and the Washington Monument in Washington are both made of marble.

True

37. Some stars are nearer to us than the sun.

False: The sun is only 93,000,000 miles away, but the nearest star is about four and a half light years away.

38. High-heeled shoes are an invention of the twentieth century.

False: High-heeled shoes have been the fashion at various times in the history of man. Gentlemen used to wear them with their silk-and-lace knee breeches.

39. Selvage is the scraps of material which are saved and later used in making rugs.

False: Selvage is the woven edge of a fabric, which will not ravel.

40. Benjamin Franklin invented the sewing machine.

False: Elias Howe is credited with inventing the sewing machine in the nineteenth century.

41. All edible nuts grow on trees.

False: Peanuts grow on small plants and have to be dug out of the ground.

42. The average adult has fifty-two teeth.

False: Thirty-two is the average number.

43. The United States Capitol Building in Washington was completed in two years.

False: It took almost seventy years to complete it.

44. The Julian Calendar is the official calendar of the United States.

False: The Gregorian Calendar is used in most civilized countries.

45. All adverbs end in "ly."

False: Near and far are adverbs.

46. A polygon is a man who has many wives.

False: A polygon is a many-sided figure.

47. Water is brought great distances by viaducts.

False: Aqueducts bring water great distances. Viaducts are bridgelike structures over ravines or valleys.

48. Seven stars form the outline of the Big Dipper.

True

49. A momentum is a token of remembrance.

False: That's a memento. Momentum is the force possessed by an object in motion.

50. When the supply of goods exceeds the demand, the market is said to be a "buyer's market."

    True: The buyer has a chance to force a price to his advantage.

51. The Zodiac is divided into twelve sections.

    True: There are twelve Signs of the Zodiac, named after twelve constellations.

52. Hartford, Connecticut, is noted as an insurance center.

    True: A number of insurance companies have their home offices there.

53. A cartographer works on maps and charts.

    True

54. Percale is a leafy green vegetable.

    False: Percale is a fine cotton fabric.

55. On a ship, the port lights are always blue.

    False: Red signifies the port side.

56. Norway is separated from Sweden by the Baltic Sea.

    False: Both Norway and Sweden are on the mainland of the Scandinavian Peninsula. They're separated by a mountain range.

57. The West Indies are east of the North American Continent.

    True

58. An abrasion is a slight bruise.

    False: The skin is broken when you have an abrasion.

59. The even-numbered pages of a book are usually on the left-hand side.

    True

60. *A Tale of Two Cities* by Dickens is the story of Rome and Florence.

    False: It's about Paris and London.

61. According to an old nursery rhyme, Jack Spratt ate only lean meat.
    True
62. Lincoln delivered the Gettysburg Address for the purpose of dedicating a library.
    False: He made it at the dedication of a cemetery.
63. The more air forced into a basketball the lighter it gets.
    False: It becomes heavier.
64. A good firm bridge hand is important in the game of billiards.
    True: It's the position of the hand on the table.
65. All news reporters are members of the Fourth Estate.
    True: It's the name often given to the press.
66. Robert Browning died in early youth.
    False: He lived to be seventy-seven.
67. Fish sometimes drown.
    True: When they are unable to get the proper amount of oxygen from the water
68. Fish often sleep with their eyes open.
    True
69. When an eight-cylinder car is in good condition, all of the eight cylinders hit at once.
    False: They alternate in groups, depending upon the make of the car.
70. Railroad ties are usually more than four feet long.
    True: They are eight to nine feet long.
71. Almost all substances have the same boiling point.
    False: No two substances have the same boiling point.
72. The United States uses more soap than any other country in the world.
    True: The United States uses one third of all the soap made.

73. A pound of feathers weighs less than a pound of iron.
    False: Both would be equal.

74. Chemists often use alcohol to dry their test tubes.
    True: The alcohol absorbs any moisture that may be in the tubes.

75. Air can be liquefied.
    True: It can be compressed until it becomes liquid.

76. A sawyer is a wood cutter.
    True

77. A two-by-four means a piece of lumber two feet wide and four feet long.
    False: It means a piece two inches thick and four inches wide, but any length.

78. Many British newspapers run advertisements on the front page.
    True

79. All newspapers use eight columns to a page.
    False: Many have less—4, 5, 7, etc.

80. The United States has a national system of education.
    False: Education is controlled by state, county, and city governments. The chief function of the United States Office of Education is to collect and give out information.

81. Most railroad cars are wider than the track.
    True

82. The portrait of Alexander Hamilton appears on all United States ten-dollar bills made within the last ten years.
    True: All bills of the same denomination bear the same portrait and Alexander Hamilton is the man whose picture is on a ten.

83. The plane "The Spirit of St. Louis" is kept in St. Louis.
    False: It's hanging in the Smithsonian Institute in Washington, D.C.

84. The "Mona Lisa" was painted by Leonardo da Vinci.
True: It's one of Leonardo da Vinci's greatest works.

85. In horse racing, if you bet on a horse to show, you can collect if he comes in second.
True: You collect if he comes in first, second, or third.

86. In lawn tennis, the court is made longer for doubles than for singles.
False: It's made wider.

87. The world-famous "Toreador Song" comes from the opera "Carmen."
True

88. There is water in an opal.
True: Two to thirteen per cent of the stone is water. This accounts for the prismatic colors.

89. Loch Lomond is a beautiful blue lake in Ireland.
False: It's in Scotland.

90. The cry "Fifty-four forty or fight!" was a Presidential campaign slogan.
True: It was used during the Presidential campaign of James Polk in 1844.

91. In aviation, RPM means radio operator, pilot, and mechanic.
False: RPM stands for revolutions per minute.

92. Douglas Corrigan's famous wrong-way flight was from Honolulu to Los Angeles.
False: His wrong-way flight was from New York to Ireland.

93. Cambric tea is made from the leaves of the cambric tree.
False: It's made of sweetened hot water and milk.

94. In baseball, the catcher may wear any kind of mitt he wishes.

True

95. According to the famous poem, the mighty Casey was playing in the Yankee Stadium when he struck out.

False: He was playing in Mudville.

96. The vanilla plant from which we get vanilla flavoring is a member of the orchid family.

True: The vanilla is a tall, clinging orchid plant with fragrant flowers.

97. Batters have to run a quarter of a mile when they hit a home run.

False: It's only 360 feet around the bases.

98. Cornucopias bloom in winter time.

False: They're paper or cardboard horns for holding candy or fruit.

99. The ancient Egyptians grew roses.

True: Roses have been found in the dry bouquets taken from Egyptian tombs.

100. A snake plant coils up at night.

False: The leaves or spikes remain upright.

Forbidden Letter

You will need: 6 or more players
Half an hour's playing time

Players can be seated in any order around the room. The host announces that he doesn't like some letter of the alphabet such as L and that when he asks each guest a question it must be answered without any word using this letter. Answers must make sense, even though L does have to be avoided.

Any player who cannot answer a question or forgets and uses the letter L has a point charged against him. When the host has asked each guest a question, another player chooses a different letter to be avoided and the game proceeds. The host or person asking the questions can use the forbidden letter as often as he wishes. Scoring is made on mistakes only, so the player with the lowest score wins.

Questions and answers might go something like this, if L is the forbidden letter:

HOST: Bill, is it a lawyer or a doctor who usually draws up a will?

BILL: Attorneys.

HOST: Evelyn, what is the fruit that is small, yellow, and sour?

EVELYN: It's one of the citrus fruits.

HOST: What do you hit at when you're playing golf, George?

GEORGE: An object known as "that darned white sphere."

Etc.

What Is It?

You will need: 10 or more players
At least half an hour's playing time
20 to 25 objects with a firm, distinctive shape
Scraps of cloth to tie them in
Pencil and paper for each guest

This is a game that can be played with a definite time limit or off and on throughout the evening. Either way it takes a good deal of feeling on the part of your guests before they can determine the identity of the objects. If the players number less than ten, have them work individually. But for more than ten, guessing in teams of two is usually more successful.

Before the party, take a short tour around the house, through your pockets, and even into the food closet, selecting as you go everyday objects with a distinctive shape. These might include the following:

An electric light bulb
A lipstick case
A package of cigarettes (with the cellophane wrapper removed)
A spool of thread
An onion, orange, or lemon
A carrot, potato, or green pepper
A small candle (table, not birthday, size)
A compact
An empty salt cellar
A fifty-cent piece
A bar of soap
A nail brush
An empty eyeglass case
A small battery (flashlight size)
A can of paste-type shoe polish
A large-size nut, such as a walnut
A large-sized bottle cork
A man's shaving brush
A package of gum or life savers
A small rubber ball or a golf, tennis, or ping pong ball

Having collected your objects, tie them in individual cloth sacks—old napkins, dish towels, or any scrap of material will do for this as long as it is not transparent material. Number each bag and make a list according to these numbers as you wrap, so that you are not confused as to the contents of each sack.

Players are provided with pencil and paper. They list, by number, the results of their feelings. The guest or team with the highest number of correct guesses wins.

I Am Going to Duluth

You will need: 6 or more players
15 minutes' playing time

The host turns to one of the players and says, "John, I am going to Duluth." The host immediately starts to count to ten and before he reaches that number, John must call out the names of three things beginning with the letter D, such as Dolls, Doughnuts, Dresses. If he succeeds in naming three things, the host turns to another guest and names another city. Whoever cannot name three objects beginning with the first letter of the city mentioned must in turn become the questioner.

Rogues' Gallery

You will need: 8 or more players
20 to 30 minutes' playing time
Magazine or newspaper pictures of 20 famous people in the current news
A sheet of paper for each picture
Pencil and paper for each guest

Go through magazines and newspapers looking for pictures of famous people famous in current news. Pictures in which these people are performing some unusual action, or wearing clothing apart from their usual custom, will make the guessing more difficult.

Cut out each picture, being careful to clip off everything which might disclose the person's identity. The pictures are then mounted on sheets of paper and each is numbered. These can be pinned to a drapery, or mounted on a large cardboard and hung on the wall.

Guests number their papers and try to fill in the names of the people in your Rogues' Gallery. You may have a set playing time for this game, or play it as one to which guests go back during lulls in the evening. The player with the most correct answers wins.

This Is My Nose

You will need: 8 or more players
10 minutes' playing time

Guests are seated for this game. The host points to one part of his body and at the same time says it is something else. When he calls a guest by name, that player must immediately touch whatever part of his body the host named and say it is another part. Play continues around to the left of the first player called. The game must go rapidly in order to be successful. Any player who hesitates, fails to touch the part of the body named by the preceding player, or does not mention another part of his own body is charged with a mistake. Two mistakes eliminate a guest from the play. The game might go like this:

HOST (touching his ear): This is my nose, Bill.
BILL (touching his ear): This is my heel, Pat.
PAT (touching her heel): This is my eye, Dora.
DORA (touching her eye): This is my eye. (Mistake)

Dora is charged with one mistake and the person on her left continues the game.

Proverbs

You will need: 8 or more players
Half an hour's playing time

The proverbs and sayings people say almost unconsciously each day are hard to remember in the middle of a game, as your guests will discover when they play Proverbs.

The players are divided into two teams and take their positions at opposite ends of the room. The first player of one team calls the name of any player on the opposing side and immediately starts to count to 15. The player whose name was called must repeat a proverb before the counter reaches that number.

If he succeeds, then it is his turn to ask for a proverb. If he fails he leaves his group and joins the other team as a prisoner. No proverb can be repeated, and the game continues until one team has taken over all the players on the opposing team.

See list of proverbs on page 37.

Observation

You will need: 6 or more players
10 minutes' playing time
25 assorted objects
Pencil and paper for each guest

Before the party, gather any twenty-five miscellaneous objects and keep them out of sight until the start of the game. Distribute pencil and paper to each guest and ask all players to close their eyes while you arrange the twenty-five objects in the center of the floor.

At the signal to look, guests are given two full minutes to study the twenty-five objects. At the end of this time, cover the grouping on the floor with a blanket, coat, or sheet and ask the players to list each thing they have observed.

Five minutes are allowed for listing everything remembered. Then the host uncovers the twenty-five objects. One point is scored for each correct object listed, and two points subtracted for anything listed which is not in the group. Player with the highest score wins.

An ash tray
A fountain pen
A framed picture
A loose snapshot
A box of cereal
A can of soup
A dish towel
A terry-cloth towel

A spool of thread
A pair of scissors
A box of candy
A box of soap flakes
An electric cord
A ball of string
A wooden mixing spoon
A carving knife
A book of matches
A yellow pencil
A pencil of another color
A book
A fifty-cent piece
A quarter
A coat hanger
An electric-light bulb
A can opener
A penknife
A screw driver or hammer

Tree Leaves

You will need: 6 or more players
15 minutes' playing time
Photographs or drawings of 10 different leaves
Pencil and paper for each guest

This is a difficult guessing game, for not many people can recognize more than three or four leaves. If you can collect ten actual leaves of different varieties in your own neighborhood, that is fine. If not, photographs or simple outline drawings will do just as well. Mount the leaves or pictures on paper and number each.

Players are given pencil and paper, and try to identify each leaf. If you have more than 10 guests, have them work in teams, for this is a game in which combined knowledge will be very helpful.

Fizz Baseball

You will need: 10 or more players
Half an hour's playing time
4 magazines or books to mark the bases
Pencil and paper for scoring

Books or magazines are placed on the floor to simulate home plate and first, second, and third bases. The host acts as umpire and scorekeeper.

Guests are divided into two teams and take their positions, one in the field and one at bat. The team in the field selects one man as pitcher and the other members of that team seat themselves in any order. They must count in that order throughout the game.

The pitcher takes his place in the mound in the center of the room and the first member of the batting team takes his place at home plate. Others on the batting team have agreed on a counting order which they too must maintain throughout the game.

The pitcher calls any number from 1 through 9, which then becomes the forbidden number. Whenever the counting reaches that number, a multiple of it, or a number in which it appears, the player whose turn it is must say "Fizz" instead of the number.

If, for example, the pitcher calls the number 4, the batter would say the next number, 5, and the counting then goes down his line of teammates like this: "6, 7, Fizz, 9, 10, 11, Fizz, 13, Fizz, 15, Fizz, etc.

If a man on the batting team makes a mistake, or hesitates too long, the batter is out and a second batter takes his place. If the batting team gets through without a mistake, the counting immediately goes back to the fielding team, starting with the pitcher and then going on through his teammates. If a member of the fielding team makes a mistake, the batter advances one base and another player replaces him at home plate. The pitcher can change the number with each new batter.

If the counting goes through both teams without a mistake being made, the batter is automatically out and is replaced at bat by another member of his team. Scoring is kept just as in baseball, with three outs to each half of an inning.

The counting must go rapidly. Any hesitation counts as a mistake, with the umpire allowing the batter a base if the hesitation is on the part of the fielding team, or calling the batter out if a player of the team at bat is too slow with his count.

My Grandmother's Trunk

You will need: 6 or more players
15 minutes' playing time

For generations, My Grandmother's Trunk has been the test of a good memory and the ability to keep a straight face, for not only does the player have to repeat an ever-increasing list of objects, but he must do so without smiling or laughing.

The guests are seated. The host starts the game by saying "My Grandmother keeps andirons in her trunk." The guest on his left must repeat this and then add an object beginning with the letter B, such as beans. The third player repeats both andirons and beans and then adds a third object beginning with the letter C.

Play continues around the room with each guest repeating the entire list already named and then adding an object for the next letter of the alphabet. Anyone who leaves out an object, or smiles or laughs while he is repeating the list, is eliminated from the game.

What's the Product?

You will need: 6 or more players
15 minutes' playing time
A list of 20 advertising slogans
Pencil and paper for each guest

Before the party, select twenty well-known advertising slogans from magazines and newspapers or radio and television programs and number each.

Guests are provided with pencil and paper and copy each slogan and number as you read it aloud. Allow fifteen minutes for each guest to match each slogan to the product it advertises. The player with the most correct guesses wins.

SLOGANS

They satisfy	Chesterfield
Not one case of throat irritation due to smoking ———	Camels
For that smoother taste—just ask for	Pabst Blue Ribbon Beer
Fast help for headache	Bromo Seltzer
Fresh-up with ———————	Seven Up
Keep your whole mouth wholesome	Ipana
Be happy go lucky	Lucky Strike
How mild can a cigarette be?	Camels
Known by the company it keeps	Seagram's V O
A treat instead of a treatment	Old Gold
Not a cough in a carload	Old Gold
Soup for lunch	Campbell's
Better buy ———	Buick

It's flaky! It's tender! It's made with	Crisco
Someone you love is hoping for a	Hamilton
Now—shaving at its best	Schick
Give your car a flying horse-power lift	Mobilgas
57 different varieties	Heinz
We dare them all	Philip Morris
The man of distinction	Lord Calvert

Billboard

You will need: 8 or more players
20 minutes' playing time
20 magazine or newspaper advertisements
Pencil and paper for each guest

This is a variation of What's the Product? in which you use the advertisement without the slogan. Before the party, cut twenty well-known ads from magazines or newspapers and carefully clip away anything which reveals the name of the product.

Paste them on separate sheets of paper and number each, or mount them on one large piece of cardboard with a number below each advertisement. Guests either play this as a fill-in game to which they may return at any point in the evening or try to guess the product advertised within a time limit of twenty minutes. The player with the greatest number of correctly identified products wins.

The Number Game

You will need: 8 or more players
Half an hour's playing time

Played to a rhythm of clapping hands together for three counts and then snapping the fingers high in the air on the fourth beat, this is a fast-rhythm game which can be started any time all the guests are seated.

Each chair in which a guest is seated is given a number, starting with the host's chair as No. 1 and then in order around the room to his right. No matter who is sitting in it, the chair will retain that number throughout the game.

The host starts the rhythm and when everyone is beating it together waits for the fourth beat and then calls a number such as 8. On the next fourth beat, the player in Seat 8 must call out another number, perhaps 2. If a player fails to answer his seat number by calling another, or answers on anything but the fourth beat, he is charged with a mistake and must go to the seat with the highest number. All other players who were after the guest making a mistake then move up one place. These players must now answer to a new number, that of the new chair in which they are sitting.

The speed of the game depends upon the speed of the rhythm and it is important that this be maintained even after players have had to change places several times and are less likely to recall their current numbers. Players try to reach Seat 1 and stay there as long as possible.

Three Words

You will need: 6 or more players
20 to 30 minutes' playing time
A soft rubber or ping pong ball

Players can be seated in any order around the room. The host tosses a ball or tightly rolled napkin to one of the guests, says some three-letter word, and immediately starts counting to 10.

The player to whom the ball is thrown must, before the host reaches 10, say three words, each one beginning with a different letter in the word called by the host. If he fails to do this, he throws the ball to another guest and calls a word. But if he succeeds, he returns the ball to the host, who tries another player. The game might go like this:

HOST (throwing ball to Mary): BID—1, 2, 3, 4, etc.
MARY (catching ball): Bird, idiot, dog.
HOST (throwing ball to Henry): CAT—1, 2, 3, 4, etc.
HENRY (catching ball): Can, at, to.

Sportsman's Row

You will need: 8 or more players
15 minutes' playing time
15 pictures of famous athletes
Pencil and paper for each guest

Strictly for those who follow sports, this game can be made as difficult as you wish. Newspapers and magazines will furnish photographs of current athletic stars. Clip these, cutting off the names, and mount each picture on a numbered piece of paper.

Guests try to identify each athlete by name within the 15

minutes' playing time allowed. The player with the highest number of correct guesses wins.

Pictures for Sportsman's Row may include all types of athletic stars, but if the time of year or your guests indicate the mood for specialization, try a series of pictures on football, baseball, hockey, or tennis players currently in the news.

What Dropped?

You will need: 8 or more players
20 minutes' playing time
15 unbreakable objects
A folding screen or sheet

What Dropped? is an easy game—for you. All you do is stand behind a screen or sheet and drop things on the floor while the guests answer the question "What dropped?"

Before the party, assemble about fifteen unbreakable objects from around the house. Keep these hidden until it is time for the game to start and then establish yourself—and the objects—behind a screen, but within easy hearing distance of the guests.

Players are provided with pencils and paper, on which they list from one to fifteen. One by one you drop the articles, allowing at least thirty seconds after each for the guests to try and determine just what it is you dropped. If there is a request to do so, drop the same object again. The player with the greatest number of correct guesses wins. If two or more guests have guessed the object, but one is more accurate than the others, he is the one to get the point.

The objects to be dropped might include:

A piece of table silver
A key ring with keys
A ping pong ball
A wet dishcloth
A man's shoe
A large kitchen knife

A deck of cards
A potato
A pot cover
A pin
A newspaper
Five pennies
A thick magazine
A pencil

How Many?

You will need: 8 or more players
15 minutes' playing time
10 articles of varying weights, lengths, or sizes
Paper and pencil for each guest

This game must be planned before the guests arrive. Select 10 to 15 articles and for each write a question as to how much it weighs, how long it is, or how much its capacity is.

Number each object and tape the accompanying question to it. During any quiet periods of the evening, or for the 15 minutes' allotted playing time, guests look at each article and try to guess the answers to the questions. These are recorded on the paper given to each player. The guest whose answers come closest to the correct ones wins.

Articles and questions to select might be:

A very thick book. How many pages?
A partially filled gallon jug. How many gills does it contain?
A paper of common pins. How many pins in the paper?
A table lamp. How many inches high?
A partially filled canister of sugar. How much does it weigh?
A small jar of dried beans. How many beans in the jar?
A ball of string. How many yards?
A big wad of cotton. How much does it weigh?
A partially used pencil. How many inches long?
A stack of writing paper. How many sheets?
A box of small buttons. How many buttons?

A head of cabbage, lettuce, or cauliflower. How much does it weigh?
A dish of raisins. How many?
A bunch of toothpicks held with a rubber band. How many toothpicks?
A ball. The circumference?

What's the Scoop?

You will need: 6 or more players
45 minutes' playing time
Unlined paper and pencil for each guest
A list of current news events

Guests are divided into two teams. If any of the players have artistic ability, try to divide the talented ones evenly between the teams. Each player is provided with several sheets of plain paper and a pencil. The host writes out some event currently in the news and gives it to one team to illustrate. Each player may take a part of the event, so that when they are finished the four or five single drawings will illustrate the complete event, or each guest may draw the whole thing himself.

The host gives the opposing team a different piece of news to draw and then all players are allowed ten minutes to complete their pictures. At the end of that period the teams exchange drawings and try to guess the news story from the pictures.

The events to be drawn may be as simple or as complicated as you wish. For example, you might give one team a story like this:

> At 11 o'clock this morning a truck from Brown's Grocery store collided with a school bus at the intersection of Linden and Maple Streets. A passenger car driven by

an unidentified woman ran into the rear of the bus. At the time of the crash the policeman on duty at the intersection was chasing a man who had stolen a string of hot dogs from Morgan's Meat Store.

Team members must then include in their drawings a clock with hands pointing to 11; a sun to indicate daytime; a truck with the name of the store; a bus lettered SCHOOL BUS. They must show street signs with the proper names, a passenger car at the rear of the bus, a policeman running down the street, the man with the string of frankfurters, and a sign for Morgan's Meat Store.

Acting Rhymes

You will need: 8 or more players
30 minutes' playing time

The guests are divided into two teams. The first team goes into another room and decides on a word it wants the other players to guess. When they return, each member acts out a word which rhymes with the selected word. From their actions the guessing team tries to determine the proper word. If, for example, the acting team decides on the word *pit,* one player might come into the room and *sit* down on the floor. Another player would pretend to catch a ball in a baseball *mitt.* A third player would go through the motions of trying on a shoe to make it *fit.* Another guest might pretend to *hit* someone. No props are allowed.

The guessing team get five points if they guess the word within three minutes. It is then their turn to act out a rhyme.

Word Rhymes

You will need: 8 or more players
Half an hour's playing time

This is another rhyme game, which is played with one group instead of teams. The host starts with a word and the player to his left must fill in with a word that rhymes with the host's word. This continues around the room until it reaches a player who cannot think of a rhyming word. This player is charged with one mistake and starts another word. Three mistakes eliminate a player from the game.

8. *For the Energetic*

RACES, relays, and games of action, these will satisfy the energetic, but still maintain the solidity of your living-room walls. These games require moving around and activity, but there isn't one that is too active for the limits of the average-sized house or apartment.

Pass the Hot Potato

You will need: At least 10 players
About 15 minutes' playing time
Record player, musical radio program, or piano
Potatoes for all guests but one

This game is a farfetched variation of musical chairs. All the guests get on their knees on the floor in a circle. All but one has a potato under his right hand. When the host or hostess starts the music, the players pass the potato to the person on the left. The object is to try and have a potato in your hand when the music stops. The one without a potato is eliminated and one potato is withdrawn. The game can continue until only one person is left.

Number Relay

You will need: At least 10 or 12 players
About 20 minutes to a half hour's playing time
2 charts with numbers on them from 1 to 31
A black crayon for each team

Before the party, two large charts consisting of about 100 numbers from 1 to 31 are prepared. These can be cut from a large wall calendar or printed very plainly in black crayon. The numbers should be all mixed up and not in numerical order.

The guests are divided into two teams. Each team is given a black crayon and stands about 8 or 10 feet from the chart in single file with their backs to it.

The host has made a list of numbers which coincide with the numbers on the chart but are not in the same order. When he calls the first number, the guest nearest the chart turns around, runs to the chart, and as quickly as possible crosses out the number that has been called. He runs back and hands the crayon to the next person in line. When the host sees the first number crossed out he calls the second one. He does not repeat the calls.

The winning team is the one that crosses out all the numbers first with the fewest mistakes. If a mistake is made, the person who made it must go back and correct it before the next one can continue the relay.

Balance the Egg

You will need: At least 10 or 12 players
About 10 or 15 minutes' playing time
One hard-boiled egg for each team
A spoon for each player

Two teams are formed and face each other. Everybody has a spoon which is held by the handle between his teeth. An egg is put on the spoon of the first person on each team and the object is to get the egg to the end of the line first. No hands are allowed and there can be some close calls. Do not tell the guests ahead of time that the eggs are hard-boiled.

Blow Fish

You will need: About 8 players
About 10 or 15 minutes' playing time
Two celluloid fish of different colors
A dishpan

A large dishpan is filled with water and a celluloid fish is placed at each end of the pan. The object of the game is to blow your fish across the pan first. One couple races at a time. The losers are eliminated and the winners then race against each other.

Balloon Volley Ball

You will need: At least 10 or 12 players
About 15 or 20 minutes' playing time
A balloon (maybe two, for good measure)
A sheet

The guests are divided into two teams. A sheet is held or supported by two less energetic guests. The players get on their knees and the game starts. The scoring can be like a simplified volley ball, but the players are so close together there is no need for any change of positions. The first team to score ten points is the winner.

Fruit Relay

You will need: At least 10 or 12 players
About 15 or 20 minutes' playing time
A lemon or an orange and a pencil for each team

The guests are divided into two groups and lined up on the same side of the room. A line is marked off on the other side of the room and the object of the game is for each player to roll the fruit, using only a pencil, to this line and back. Then the next team member takes the pencil and does the same thing. The winning team is the one whose last player comes over the finish line first.

Pin Boy

You will need: At least 10 or 12 players
About 15 minutes' playing time
Five bottles (small variety, like Coca-Cola or beer bottles)
A rubber ball

All the guests with the exception of one form a circle around the room. The five bottles are placed on markers in the center of the circle and one person is IT. One of the players in the ring throws the ball, trying to hit the bottles. Whether he does or not, the ball will roll across to another player, who must try to hit the bottles. When some or all of the bottles are knocked down IT must put all of them back on the markers before another player throws. If he does this, the last person to throw the ball becomes IT. If not, the same person stays in the center of the circle until he succeeds in this.

Olympics

You will need: At least 10 or 12 players
About 15 minutes' playing time
2 pieces of string and 2 funnels made of paper

Two teams are picked from the group of guests. The two pieces of string, about chin high and several yards apart, are stretched across the room. Paper funnels are shaped around each of these pieces of string. Each team is divided in two with half at one end of the string and half at the other. One team member blows the funnel to the far end of the string and the second member, who is waiting there, blows the funnel back to the third member. The winning team is the first one to complete the relay.

In the Air

You will need: At least 10 or 12 players
About 15 minutes' playing time
A feather or a fluffy piece of cotton for each team

The guests are divided into two teams and a goal is set part way across the room. The first player on each team is given a feather or a small piece of fluffy cotton, which he blows to the goal line. Once there, he can grab it and run back to hand it to the next person in line. The winning team is the one to finish the race with the fewest marks against it (touching the feather before the goal is reached, letting it hit the ground).

The Necktie Race

You will need: At least 10 or 12 players
About 15 or 20 minutes' playing time
A necktie for each side

Two teams are picked from the guests and are lined up facing each other. The first player in each line has a necktie, which he must tie around his neck with a regular knot. He must then shake hands with the player on his right, untie the tie, and hand it to the next player, who does the same thing. If the women are spread out evenly on both sides, that adds to the confusion and the laughs—also the handicaps.

The winning team is the one that completes this procedure of tying, shaking hands, and untying with the fewest team members unable to tie a regular knot.

Hoop-la

You will need: At least 10 or 12 players
About 15 minutes' playing time
A finger ring for each team, or a lifesaver
A toothpick for each guest

The guests are divided into two or more teams, depending on the number of players. The team members stand side by side, each one with a toothpick in his mouth. The object of the race is to pass the ring or lifesaver as quickly as possible down the line and back. If it is dropped on the way down the line, it must start over again at the beginning. If the ring or lifesaver is dropped on the return trip, it must start at the foot of the line.

Line-up

You will need: At least 12 players
About 15 minutes' playing time
5-inch-square cardboards for each player

The guests are divided into two teams and two sets of numbers are made which cover the number of players on each team. The host is seated at the opposite end of the room and when a number of two, three, or four digits is called, the players holding these cards run to the other end of the room and take their proper places in front of the host to form the number he has called. A point is given to the team that first completes each number. The winning team is the first one to get twelve points.

Leading the Blind

You will need: About 10 players
Blindfolds
About 10 to 15 minutes' playing time

Each team is made up of two men and a girl. The two men are blindfolded and it's the girl's job to lead the men through a course and back to the finishing line without having them fall or take off their blindfolds.

The girl stands in front of the two men and stretches her hands in back of her for them to grab. The turning point of the course may be a chair, which will slow them up in getting around it.

If there is any need for the game to get more confused, the teams can skip over their course.

Full Dress Relay

You will need: About 12 players
About 15 minutes' playing time
A large suitcase for each team
Dress-ups for each team like galoshes, a hat, a huge skirt, large-sized slacks and shirt, men's shoes for the women, etc.

The guests are divided into two teams, half on one side of the room and half on the other. Each couple is given a suitcase full of clothes, certain ones for the girl and certain ones for the man. At the starting line they open the suitcase, put on the specified clothing, close the suitcase, and, the man carrying the suitcase, run to the other end of the room, where there is another couple of the same team waiting. The first couple take off the clothes, put them back in the suitcase, and hand it to the next couple, who open it, put on the clothes, rush to the other end of the room, take them off, put them back in the suitcase, close it, and hand it to the next couple. This continues until all the couples have completed the relay. The first team to finish undressing, packing the clothes, and going over the finish line is the winner.

The Streamer Race

You will need: At least 8 or 10 people
About 15 minutes' playing time
Streamers eight or ten feet long and one inch wide
A pair of scissors for each couple

Each couple is given a paper streamer about eight or ten feet long and one inch wide and a pair of scissors. The streamer can be held at one end by one of the partners, or can be pinned to a piece of furniture. The starting signal is given and the girls start cutting first. The winner is the first one to cut all the way through to the end of the streamer. If anyone cuts through the edge, she is automatically disqualified. After the girls have a try, then it's the men s chance. The winners race against each other and narrow it down to the final winner.

Jail

You will need: At least 6 couples
About 15 or 20 minutes' playing time

Guests are seated in couples around the room, some with their backs to others, some sideways. One couple is seated in the middle of the room in two chairs known as "Jail." Each couple is given a number and when the leader calls Number 2, 3, and 4 these three couples have to change chairs and at the same time the couple in Jail tries to grab another couple's spot out of Jail. The call "Jail Break" means that every couple must change chairs.

Partners must keep their arms linked so that if a man is ahead of his partner and sees a chair, he must remember that she must find a chair that will allow them to have their arms linked. The position of the chairs can be changed after each round to make the game as difficult as possible.

Carry Your Chair

You will need: At least 10 or 12 people
About 15 minutes' playing time
A folding chair for each team

Guests are divided into two teams. The first player on each team is given a folding chair. When the signal is given, he takes his folding chair and heads for the goal at the other end of the room. When he gets there he unfolds the chair, sits down on it, gets up, folds up the chair, and runs back to the starting line, where the chair is handed to the next man on the team. The winning team is the one whose last player completes this routine first.

The Big Stretch

You will need: At least 10 or 12 people
About 10 or 15 minutes' playing time
2 circles of heavy elastic

Two teams are formed, either all men or both men and women, if the girls are "game." The heavy elastic should be just small enough so that the average person would have to do a little pulling and tugging to get it over his body.

The game starts with the first person on each team running to the far end of the room, where two large elastic bands have been placed on a chair, one for each of them. They put the elastic bands over their heads, pull them down, and step out of them. The bands are then put back on the chairs and the players rush back to touch their next teammates, so they may do the same thing.

Get the Marshmallow

You will need: At least 10 people
About 15 or 20 minutes' playing time
A string about four feet long with a marshmallow tied in the middle of it

Guests are divided into teams of two. The marshmallow is tied in the middle of the string. Teammates face each other with the string ends in their mouths. At the starting signal they try to get the marshmallow without using their hands. The first person to get the marshmallow is the winner.

Peanuts

You will need: At least 12 players
About 10 or 15 minutes' playing time
2 pans for each team
About 25 peanuts for each team

Two teams are formed in two facing lines, with a pan of peanuts beside the first player on each side and an empty pan at the end of each line. The team members clasp hands and must keep them clasped while the race is going on. The first player leans over and picks a peanut out of the pan and passes it to the person next to him, she to the next, and so on down the line. If a peanut is dropped it must be picked up with the hands clasped. The winning team is the one that first passes all the peanuts from one pan to the other.

Cracker Crumbs

You will need: At least 10 players
About 15 minutes' playing time
Saltine-like crackers

The group is broken up into two teams and each member of each team is given a cracker. When the starting signal is given, the first one on each team starts eating his cracker. The second member can't start until the first one has finished and can whistle so everyone can hear. The row finishing first gives one long whistle in unison.

Applesauce

You will need: About 8 or 10 players
About 10 or 15 minutes' playing time
An apple for each team

The guests are divided into groups of about 4 or 5 people. Each group has an apple. The first one in the line peels it, the second one cuts it in halves, the third one quarters it, the fourth one cuts out the core, and the fifth one eats it. If there aren't enough team members for each of these steps, one person could do two of them.

Eggshell Hockey

You will need: At least 8 players
About 10 or 15 minutes' playing time
One eggshell
Table with dividing line in the middle

The so-called puck is made by blowing out an egg. Guests are divided into two teams, one team at each end of a medium-sized table. A mark of some kind is drawn to show the middle of the table. The object of the game is to blow the egg so that it will go over the line toward the other team's side. Each time a team can do this a point is scored for them. A point is scored against a team if one of its players touches the egg or the table. A limit of points or time may be put on the game.

Under the Pole

You will need: At least 7 or 8 couples
About half an hour's playing time
Two supporting poles with a pole across, held up by a series of nails on the vertical poles

This game calls for old clothes and good sports. The idea is for each couple to go under the pole, one couple at a time, without knocking it down. The first round starts with the cross bar high enough so that anyone who isn't too careless can get under it without any trouble. The nails are hammered into the far side of the supporting poles, about one inch apart. It is arranged this way so that any contact with the cross bar will knock it down.

The first couple start under the pole and they must hold hands from the beginning until they get out on the other side safely. The second couple go under, the third, and so on until everyone has completed the first round, or been eliminated for knocking the bar down. Then the cross bar is moved down one notch and the second round starts. This continues until the bar is just a few inches from the floor. This is when the fun begins. Sometimes it is necessary to let your partner squirm through ahead of you, but you must hold one hand the entire time. If one gets through, he can grab the second hand and pull his partner through while she keeps perfectly flat. It's the squirming that gets those elbows out of place or makes you forget to turn your feet sideways just as you're coming through the last inch or two.

The last couple to stay in the game is the winner and you'd be surprised how often it is not necessarily the thinnest of the group.

9. The Hunt

HUNT games can be a challenge and a delight to players. They take pre-party preparation, but do not require anything you do not find in almost every house.

Camouflage

You will need: At least 10 or 12 guests
45 minutes to one hour's playing time
20 small objects (rubber band, postage stamp, etc.)
A list of these objects prepared before the party for each guest or couple

You have to prepare this game beforehand, but it doesn't take very long to do. First, you select twenty small objects which can be so placed in a room that they are actually in plain view but still difficult to see. For example: you might stick a straight pin in the back of a couch; place a rubber band in the groove of a lamp; rest a postage stamp on the bottom edge of a picture frame; put a baby's nipple on the point of a light fixture; fasten a paper clip to a curtain, or pin a safety pin in the fold of a curtain; put a piece of pencil lead in the stone of a fireplace; put a thumb tack in a chair full of hobnails; stick Scotch tape on a glass pane; put an eraser on the rung of a chair; place a button in the corner of a picture frame; stick a Band-aid on white woodwork; tie a shoe lace around a light cord, etc.

Make this observation game as difficult as you like, but for your own sake later on keep a record of where you placed everything. For the camouflage searchers, make a list of the objects (but not their hiding places) and as they discover these spots, they write down opposite the name of the object where they saw it. If the crowd is particularly large, you might have your guests search in couples.

Camouflage searchers have been known to get mighty thorough in their hunting. Safeguard your linen closet and neatly made beds by making it clear that NOTHING has to be moved or touched in order to find the things on the list. If you can hide everything in one or two rooms, that is even better.

Forty-five minutes to one hour is sufficient time to allow for hunting. Any guest or couple unable to find and write down the location of the "missing twenty" probably isn't ever going to. Once you have revealed the actual answers, be prepared for some mass movement about the room. Some people will have to prove to themselves that the pin, paper clip, elastic band, etc., are really where you say they are.

Letter Hunt

You will need: About 10 or 12 guests
About half an hour's playing time
A number of cards about 3 x 5
A six-letter word for each guest or couple

The guests are told that each of them has a six-letter word

which is hidden around the room letter by letter. The guests or couples are numbered so that guest No. 1 will know when he has found one of his letters, as it will have a No. 1 written on the back of it. If he disturbs someone else's letter, he must put it back and not tell the hiding place.

When a guest finds all his letters he must put them in the proper order to make a word. The first guest or couple to accomplish this wins.

Upside-down Scavenger Hunt

You will need: At least 12 players
About 45 minutes' playing time
A list of about 20 objects which you have put out of place
Paper and pencil for each guest

Most of us are familiar with the regular scavenger hunt, usually held outdoors, in which each couple or team is given a list of hard-to-find objects and then wanders all over the countryside trying to find them. The only similarity between that scavenger hunt and the upside-down variety is that the objects are hard to find and are obviously out of place.

At the beginning of the hunt, the host explains that twenty objects have been deliberately put out of place throughout the house or in several rooms. Guests are provided with pencil and paper and sent off to find the misplaced objects. If you have enough people, let them play by couples. The first individual or couple to complete the list of misplaced objects wins.

Your list of misplaced articles might include:

An onion mixed up with a bowl of fruit

A tape measure or shoelace used as a curtain tie

A double boiler on a bookshelf

A monkey wrench under the dining-room table

A dictionary on the kitchen table with some cookbooks
A box of salt in the living room
Celery stalks in a flower vase
Bookends as a doorstop
A bath towel for a hall rug
A strainer hanging on the living-room wall
An ashtray full of sand or dirt
Knitting in the wastebasket
A scrub mop in the living room
A can of soup on the piano
A pot cover with the records
A hot dog in place of a candle
A pill in a dish of nuts
A cigarette butt in with a box of new cigarettes
Shoes in the refrigerator
A woman's hat in the stove
A bucket of water in the fireplace

Indoor Scavenger Hunt

You will need: At least 12 players
30 minutes' playing time
A list of hard-to-find articles for each 4 guests

This is another variation of the scavenger hunt and it too may be played indoors. The host prepares lists of articles which are already in his home but would be hard for a stranger to locate. Guests hunt for these articles in teams of four and each team should have a different list so people won't be tripping over each other. Set a time limit of thirty minutes for hunting and let the players go. To keep your home in some semblance of order, it might be wise to suggest that no rifling through bureau drawers or desks is necessary. These objects should be in places that you might expect to find them—for example, an outdated newspaper would be with a pile of old newspapers in the basement or a corner of the kitchen.

The list for one team might include:

A particular magazine article
A piece of yellow yarn
A left shoe-skate
The fourth line of a particular poem
A flower for which you list the Latin name
An old license plate
A pencil stub two inches long
A jar of oregano
A recipe for shepherd's pie

A second list might include:

A bottle of green ink
A white candle
A forty-watt electric-light bulb
A bottle of French perfume for which you list the name in English
A particular record
A piece of Christmas wrapping paper
A special brand of rubber cement
Tan darning thread
Last year's appointment book
A glass that will hold a particular number of ounces

At the end of the designated hunting time, each team assembles its treasures in a pile and the winner is the team finding the most on the list.

Simple Treasure Hunt

You will need: At least 10 guests
30 to 45 minutes' playing time
A list of clues leading to the treasures

This is a simplified version of a treasure hunt in which each guest or team is given a list of clues and then tries to find the location of the object he thinks each clue indicates. Allow thirty or forty-five minutes for the guests to locate the treasures. After each clue on the list, each player tries to fill in the name of the object he has found and where he found it. When the list is completed or time is up, the person or team having the most correct answers wins.

Your clues might include:

Something in a haystack (a needle)
Something that gathers no moss (a stone)
What we hope your life doesn't hang by (a thread)
A tisket—a tasket (a basket)
For a nimble Jack (a candlestick)
Mary had one (a leg of lamb or lamb chop)
"All the world's a stage" (a volume of Shakespeare)
Merry-go-round (a recording of "Carousel")
Every letter of the alphabet (a dictionary)
There's many a slip (a cup)
Maui and Oahu (a book on Hawaii)
Guardian of the Coins (a piggy bank)
Who is fairest of them all? (a mirror)
When yellow is hot (a jar of mustard)
I burn the staff of life (a toaster)

Temp's Treasure Hunt

You will need: At least 12 guests
About an hour's playing time
A set of clues for each couple
Gummed labels
Pencils for each guest

This is a carefully worked out—and more complicated—treasure hunt, but in the version we give you here preparation time is cut by many hours because clues for six teams are already planned.

This particular hunt was organized for six couples. The same clues could be followed by teams of three members each, or by individual players if you wish a smaller party.

Before the party, write out the clues. Small gummed labels are ideal for this, as they are easy to hide and will adhere to almost any surface. Mark each clue with the team number, so there will be no confusion if Team 5 happens to find a clue designed for Team 3.

The crossword puzzle is planned as a first clue because it is a good starter. All the guests work on it in the same room and it is a part of the hunt which can be played sitting down. When all the guests have assembled, distribute pencils and the puzzle for each team. And then turn them loose.

Clues for Team 1

Players on Team 1 are given their crossword puzzle. When they have completed it, they find that the solution gives them the clue, Center Desk Drawer.

On the bottom of the desk drawer, or even underneath it, you have placed a gummed label which says Cold, Cold Cubes.

This clue leads to a refrigerator ice tray, where you have pasted a label saying Low Wooden Stand for Java.

This leads back to the living-room coffee table. In some obscure spot is a label with a series of letters which must be unscrambled. The label says LEOARPORTC.

When unscrambled, this spells Percolator. In the percolator is a label saying Hickory, Dickory Dock.

This clue leads to the bedroom clock, on the bottom of which is a label saying A Tisket, A Tasket.

TEAM 1 [Center Desk Drawer]

Horizontal

1. ——
7. Winged mammal
9. Science of ideas
11. Fish spear
12. Bring about
13. Electric Commission (Abbr.)
14. To make amends for
17. ——
19. Throw
21. Preposition
22. 7th note of scale
23. Direction
24. ——
26. Fish
27. Charge per unit
28. Lease
30. Poems
31. East Rumania (Abbr.)
32. Part of verb to be
34. Plague or contagious disease

Vertical

1. Smoker's Item
2. Publish
3. Arranges for
4. Toward
5. Elevated
6. Land measure
7. Past
8. Small nail
10. Deity
13. Pertaining to beauty
15. Negative
16. Slave, serf
18. Consumed
20. Reddish-yellow
22. Exchange
24. Let fall
25. Direction
29. Before (poetic)
33. South East

This means the kitchen wastepaper basket and here the searching couple finds the following rhyme:

FOOTBALL PLAYERS ONCE A YEAR
STAGE A MIGHTY CONTEST HERE

This leads to the sugar bowl, in which is hidden the mathematical last clue, which is the same for all teams. ON TELEVISION SET, the solution to the mathematical puzzle, leads to a label which says TREASURE.

CLUES FOR TEAM 2

Team 2 is given its crossword puzzle. When the players have completed it they find the solution gives them the clue EMPTY MATCH PACK.

Pasted on the inside of an empty match pack is a label saying IT DOESN'T TICK BUT IT KEEPS TIME.

This clue leads to an electric clock, on the bottom of which there is a label saying A DANCE CALLED "THE BIG _____"; A FLOWER CALLED _____CUP.

This leads to a jar of apple butter in the food closet. Here team members find the clue EDISON'S TABLE MODEL.

On a living-room table lamp they find a series of letters which must be unscrambled. The letters are TAMEHTSROT.

Unscrambled the letters spell THERMOSTAT. On the thermostat is a label which says LARGE BLUE RECEPTACLE FOR USED COFFIN NAILS.

This leads to a large blue ashtray and here the team members find the following rhyme:

I HAVE FOUR LEGS AND A HARD TOP, TOO.
I KNOW ALL ABOUT NUMBERS UP TO 52.

LAST CLUE FOR EVERYBODY

$\frac{24}{6} =$ FOUR

$\sqrt{81} =$ NINE

$\frac{1}{8}+\frac{1}{4}+\frac{3}{8}+\frac{1}{2}+\frac{6}{8} =$ TWO

$\frac{11 \times 84}{132} =$ SEVEN

$(120-98)-11 =$ ELEVEN

$\frac{231-126}{5} \div 7 =$ THREE

$2+7+11+10-25 =$ FIVE

$\frac{2}{3} \times \frac{63}{7} =$ SIX

$2 \times 3.5 =$ SEVEN

$(.6+.4) \times 8 =$ EIGHT

$\frac{(144 \div 12)}{3} =$ FOUR

$\frac{(2 \times 8)+4}{2} =$ TEN

$2^2+2^2-2 =$ SIX

$\frac{144-(6 \times 12)}{6} =$ TWELVE

$[(.4 \times 110)-4] \div 2 =$ TWENTY

TEAM 2 [Empty Match Pack]

1	2	3	4			5	6	7	8
9						10			
11			12	13			14		
15		16				17			
	18				19				
20					21				
			22	23			24		25
26	27	28				29		30	
31						32			
33					34				

Horizontal

1. —
5. South African plant
9. Entrance
10. Beverage
11. Advertisement
12. Grain
14. Golf mound
15. Liquefies
17. Vegetable
18. Fruit
20. Some
21. Either
22. State in U.S.
26. —
29. Tune
31. One of the Great Lakes
32. —
33. Thing done, act
34. Small islands

Vertical

1. Kind of cheese
2. Up-to-date
3. Italian river
4. Jogs
5. Part of verb to be
6. Measure of volume
7. Her cow started Chicago Fire
8. Barely make out
13. Snake
16. Put down
17. Possibly
19. Scarf of fur or feathers
20. Carried weapons
22. Cooled
23. Department of Health
24. Verbal
25. Arctic animals
27. Part of verb to be
28. Bind
30. Solid water

TEAM 3 [Hall Closet Door]

1	2	3	4		■	5	6	7	8
9				■	10				
11		■	12	13		■	14		■
15		16			■	17			18
■	19				20				
21			■	22			■	■	■
	■	■	23				24	25	26
27	28	29				■	30		
31				■	32				
■	33			■	34				

Horizontal

1. Not filled
5. —
9. —
10. A courtyard
11. Advertisement
12. A grain
14. Television
15. Liquefies
17. Max —, boxer
19. Fruit
21. Some
22. Sick
23. Science of urinary organs
27. —
30. Feather or fur scarf
31. Sharpens
32. Not wealthy
33. Married
34. Mix or mingle

Vertical

1. Kind of cheese
2. Up-to-date
3. Italian river
4. Jogs
5. Aha!, exclamation
6. Perfume from flowers
7. Organ of the body
8. Behold
10. Pint (abbr.)
13. Desires with eagerness
16. Put down
17. Gives ringing sound when struck
18. Railway (abbr.)
20. Spot or stain
21. Curve over door or window
23. Utilized
24. Wind instrument
25. Dopy fellow (slang)
26. Fenced-in area
28. Close to the ground
29. Only
32. Plural (abbr.)

This leads to the card table, on which is pasted the mathematical last clue, which is the same for all teams and leads to the television set and the word TREASURE.

CLUES FOR TEAM 3

Players on Team 3 are given their crossword puzzle. When they have completed it, they find the solution gives them the clue HALL CLOSET DOOR.

Somewhere on the door, they find a label which says 250 LOW—450 HOT.

This leads to the stove oven, in which there is a label which says A CIRCULAR REFLECTOR.

This leads to a round mirror in the bedroom and here they find a series of letters which must be unscrambled. The letters are YNODTCAIIR.

Unscrambled they spell DICTIONARY. On the flyleaf of the dictionary they find the words GOLDEN BROWN.

This leads to the toaster in the kitchen where they find a label saying MY DRAIN HAS SEEN A LOT OF DIRT.

This leads to the bathroom wash basin and here they find the following rhyme:

LONG JOHN SILVER WOULD BE FOR ME
BUT I GUARD MY TREASURE CONSTANTLY

This leads to the silver chest in which the players discover the mathematical clue which leads to the word TREASURE on the television set.

CLUES FOR TEAM 4

Players of Team 4 are given their crossword puzzle. When they have completed it, they find the solution gives them the clue KITCHEN CUPBOARD DOOR.

On one of the cupboard doors they find a label which says HANDY WHEN YOU'RE OUT OF MATCHES.

This leads to a cigarette lighter in the living room where the players find a clue saying CONTAINER FOR GREENS.

This means the salad bowl. On the bottom of the bowl there is a label which says COLD VITAMIN C.

This leads to a can of frozen orange juice and a series of letters which must be unscrambled. The letters are ELEHT-PENO.

When unscrambled this spells TELEPHONE. Pasted to some part of the phone is a label saying I'M ALWAYS UNDER WET FEET.

This leads to the bathmat, where the players find the following rhyme:

A RADIO STAR HAS BROUGHT ME FAME,
BUT NEVER MY CONTENTS HAS HE LEARNED TO TAME

This clue leads to Fibber McGee's favorite, the hall closet, in which is hidden the final mathematical clue. The solution to this puzzle leads to the television set and the label saying TREASURE.

CLUES FOR TEAM 5

Players on Team 5 are given their crossword puzzle. When completed, the solution gives them the clue EMPTY MILK BOTTLE.

In an empty milk bottle in the kitchen they find a clue which says YOU CAN LISTEN TO ME FROM MORNING TILL NIGHT.

This leads to the radio, where the players find a label reading WHAT'S HOT IN THE WINTER AND COLD IN THE SUMMER?

This clue leads to a radiator, where they discover a series of letters which must be unscrambled. The letters are EAP-RTEWPSA.

Unscrambled, this spells WASTEPAPER and in the kitchen

TEAM 4 [Kitchen Cupboard Door]

1	2	3	4	■	5		6	7	8
9				■		■	10		
11			■	12		13	■	14	
15			16		■	17	18		
19		■	20		21	■	22		
23				■	24	25		■	
26		■		■	27		■	28	
■	29	30					■	31	
32				■	■	33	34		■
35			■	■	36				

Horizontal

1. Vegetable, type of cabbage
5. Ludicrous behavior, a caper
9. False god, image
10. African antelope
11. Texas Oil Corporation
12. Meadow
14. To the top
15. Near-by
17. Woodland plant
19. Pronoun
20. Guided
22. M-G-M lion
23. Brand of gasoline
24. Preposition: Away from
26. No charge
27. Either
28. Conjunction
29. Group of nations
31. Advertisement
32. Singly
33. Be seated
35. Pigpen
36. Plural of this

Vertical

1. —
2. Growing from childhood to maturity
3. Crazy (slang—Western)
4. Elevated
5. Part of verb to be
6. Two-gun (abbr.)
7. Harden, accustom
8. —
12. Sheltered side
13. Doctor's request: "Say —"
16. Messy
18. Kind of fairy
21. —
25. New, recent
28. Grain (plural)
30. Marriage's long yoke (abbr.)
32. Bone (Latin)
34. That is

TEAM 5 [Empty Milk Bottle]

1	2	3	4		■	5	6	7	8
9				■	■	10			
11		■	12	13		■	14		
15		16			■	17			■
■	18				19				20
21			■	22			■	23	
	■	24	25			■	26	■	
27	28	■	29			30		■	
31		■	32					■	■
33				■	34				

Horizontal

1. ——
5. South African plant
9. Entrance
10. ——
11. Advertisement
12. Grain
14. Golf mound
15. Liquefies
17. Vegetable
18. Fruit
21. Girl's name
22. Electrified particle
23. Pronoun (archaic)
24. Sharp-pointed missile
27. Begone
29. Same as before
31. Boy's name
32. Insert, dental filling
33. Lease
34. Cathartic salts

Vertical

1. Kind of cheese
2. Up-to-date
3. Italian river
4. Paces
5. Morning
6. Cubic measure
7. Her cow started Chicago Fire
8. Barely make out
13. Headache cure
16. Terra firma
17. Writing instrument
19. ——
20. Period of time
21. Ire
25. Entrance
26. Playthings
28. Epic poem
30. Hit lightly

container for wastepaper the players discover a clue which says OF RUBBER OR HAIR OR DOWN I'M MADE.

This leads to a pillow, where the team members find a label saying A STITCH IN TIME SAVES NINE.

In the sewing box with the needles and thread they find the following rhyme:

OPEN THE DOOR AND LOOK RIGHT IN
WHERE THE STAFF OF LIFE IS ENCASED IN TIN

This clue leads to the breadbox, where they discover the final mathematical clue. The solution to this puzzle is ON TELEVISION SET, where the players will find the label TREASURE.

CLUES FOR TEAM 6

Players on Team 6 are given their crossword puzzle. When completed, the solution gives them the clue LIVING ROOM DOOR.

Pasted on the entrance to the living room they find a label saying ILLUMINATION FOR WRITERS.

This clue leads to the desk lamp, where there is a label which says SIX OF ONE, HALF A DOZEN OF ANOTHER—ALL IN ONE BOX.

This means the box of eggs in the refrigerator and here the players find a series of letters which must be unscrambled. The letters are KESLTACINDC.

Unscrambled, these spell CANDLESTICK. Pasted on the bottom of the candlestick is a clue saying YOU CAN SMOOTH THINGS OUT ON ME.

This leads to the ironing board, where the team members discover a clue which says LATHER HOLDER.

TEAM 6 [Living Room Door]

1	2	3	4	■	5	6	7		8
9				■	10			■	
	■		■	11				12	
13	14		15		■	16			■
17				■	18	■	19		20
■		■	■	21		22	■	23	
24		25	26		■	27	28		
29					30	■	31		■
32		■	33			34		■	35
36					■	37			

Horizontal

1. —
5. To take as one's own a child of other parents
9. One time
10. Sun
11. Lyric poems
13. Frozen rain
16. Color
17. Little ones
19. Equip
21. Small flap or tag
23. Preposition
24. Worship
27. Halt
29. —
31. Conjunction
32. Upon
33. Flower
36. Kind of heron
37. Domestic slave

Vertical

1. Method of cooking
2. On top of
3. Group of eight
4. Myself
5. Snake
6. —
7. More mature
8. Triboro Transit System
11. And (French)
12. Publisher
14. Filling with cargo
15. East Syracuse (abbr.)
18. Father
20. Republican
21. Doctrine, dogma
22. Bachelor of Science
24. Plant used as purgative and tonic
25. Old Viking (abbr.)
26. Ready for harvest
28. Playthings
30. Begone
34. Northeast
35. Us

Pasted to the bathroom soap dish they find the following rhyme:

HOLLANDAISE, CREAM SAUCE, AND PUDDINGS, TOO,
I KEEP THEM FROM BURNING RIGHT UP THE FLUE

This clue leads to the double boiler where the players discover the final mathematical clue. The solution to this puzzle is ON TELEVISION SET, where the hunters will find the word TREASURE.

10. Party Night at the Club

HERE are tips on planning, preparing, and running games for large groups. Basically, these are the same games you play at home; the important thing is to think out every detail so carefully that more than seventy-five or a hundred people may enjoy games in a club or church as much as your friends enjoy them in your living room. And if you like games, if you've seen them work in your home or the homes of friends, a club game night will be just your meat and the job will be more of a pleasure than a chore.

It starts with the committee. Mix them up, half men and half women, and keep a roving eye out for the person who has something besides interest to contribute. A man who has access to an office mimeograph machine or a typewriter can be of great help in this operation. And so can the girl who will find time in her day for a little of the leg work necessary in gathering equipment. But fundamentally, pick them because they too like games. A committee composed of six people who really believe in what they are promoting is worth twice that number in halfhearted, reluctant members.

Gather this eager group around you and if it has not already been established, set a date for the party. Three weeks is plenty of time for organizing a game night, but don't settle for much less than that if you can help it.

The invitation is the first matter to be settled. As chairman of this party you are a salesman. Take a cue from the advertising men who make selling a product theii business. Your invitation or announcement is really an ad. Be enthusiastic! Sell your party from the very start.

You can do it with a jingle on a penny postcard. You can use line drawings and a few words on a piece of mimeograph paper. You can have great, colorful posters placed in strategic spots throughout your selling area. But whatever form your announcement takes, make it clear that this is a "different" party no member can afford to miss. Just don't forget to include such practical facts as the date and time.

With invitations out of the way, the rest of your problem is much the same as it would be if you were planning a party for your home. The only difference comes in the multiplication table: you are now planning for many more players than you would ever invite to your house. This increases your responsibility really to know the games you will play and to be able to explain them well. It means you will have to have every single piece of equipment selected ahead of time, because your usual last-minute rummaging spots such as the desk drawer and kitchen cupboard will be two blocks away. But the story really isn't very grim, for you have three weeks in which to prepare.

If you know the exact number of expected guests, that's fine. If not, estimate as closely as possible and then plan for twenty more than that number just to be on the safe side.

But you can't prepare unless you know just what you're preparing for, so with the aid of your committee, select the games you want to play. And then test them!

Later on in this chapter certain games will be suggested for large groups. There are many others, possibly one that is your favorite, that would do just as well. No matter how often you've played these games, write out a set of instructions or an explanation which will make the method of play clear to someone who has never been introduced to it before. And then try these instructions on a small group. You may be a game-writing wizard and find everything is perfectly clear. There is also the possibility that you are so familiar with the game that you omit something which would be helpful to a new player. This test run on a small group will give you a chance to work on and clarify directions to the point where even the vaguest of guests will know what is supposed to happen.

Clear, explicit directions are wonderful, but sometimes a live demonstration or a few written words can be even better—and not so dull. Let the committee members become actors for a few minutes on the night of the party. A brief demonstration by them of the way to play a game may accomplish more than you could with fifteen minutes of chatter into a microphone.

Whether the games are spoken, demonstrated, or written, some games need equipment, and this is something to be collected ahead of time. A little scrounging around will produce almost everything you need. You'll be able to find many of the essentials in your house and the houses of your committee members and friends. Whatever purchases may be necessary will be of the dime-store variety and shouldn't set the budget back too much. Purchases may not be necessary at all.

Whether purchased or borrowed, all the equipment must be there before the party starts. If your games take pencil and paper, accept only the kind of pencil that comes with an already sharpened point and an eraser, for even the best of us make mistakes we'd like to correct. If you are using lots of common pins, take them out of the paper beforehand and put them all in a little box. String or paper streamers should be cut the exact length you will need. Chalk should be broken into pieces of usable size. Put all the equipment for the games into piles marked with the name of the game.

Guests at a large party are like sheep: first none arrive; then they come in twos and threes, and then they come in droves. For a good party, you have to be prepared for all stages. The twos and threes need to be made to feel welcome instead of apologetic for being on time. Have something planned for them to do. This can be a game like Spider Web or Billboard, or When I Was a Child. It really doesn't matter what it is so long as there is something for people to do while they wait for those who will come dashing in crying "The baby sitter didn't come," or "John picked tonight to miss his train."

But those who arrive late also need prompt attention. If you're not ready for them you're headed for complete confusion and your well-planned party is in danger. Being ready consists of having the hat-and-coat department under control, knowing how you are going to divide this mass of people into playable teams, and having someone with a microphone or megaphone in hand to start a game as soon as the main group of guests has arrived.

You should have your system of splitting people into teams well set up ahead of time. For some games you can have two teams of any size, but for others the guests will have a better time if there are only ten or twelve players on any one side. You can establish the division for any number of teams at the very beginning.

Do it by number or do it by color. For the number system, base all your team planning on whatever game has the fewest number of players on a side and divide this into the total number of expected guests. If, for example, you want to play a game which can have no more than eight on a team and know you will have eighty guests, you then prepare for a maximum of ten teams with eight players on each. Write the number 1 on eight small slips of paper, the number 2 on eight others, 3 on eight more, and so on until you have gone through ten. The color system is figured exactly the same way, except that you cut up eight slips of paper of one color for Team 1, eight of another color for Team 2, etc.

The numbered or colored slips are then mixed up and put in a box. As guests arrive they are presented with the box and draw a number which gives them a team membership. Naturally, you don't want the eight people on a team to be in an isolated little group by themselves all evening, so when it comes to a game which may be played with larger teams, you ask that Teams 1 and 2 combine forces against 3 and 4.

Many other combinations of teams can be worked out, because as long as you did your original figuring on the basis of the game requiring the smallest-sized teams, you will have no trouble merging them into larger groups. The only thing that matters is to decide on your system and then follow it through, so that as committee chairman you do not spend your evening either picking teams or herding backward players into some group.

Even with a number or a color to guide them, guests need some help in finding where their teams are supposed to meet. Something as simple as a large convention-type card tacked to the wall or a high pole can do this for you and save a lot of repeated directions. But do make the numbers or the letters spelling the colors large enough so that even the near-sighted lady who came without her glasses can locate home base for her team.

As with any party, you want your guests to have fun, but not to spend two hours panting for breath or two hours suffering from that peculiar fatigue which comes only from prolonged sitting. Vary the degree of activity. And vary the degree of interest you are asking of each guest. Some people can participate for just so long and then have to revert to their natural habitat of spectator. Others have to be in on everything or else they are miserable. To take care of both groups, give thought to audience appeal when you select the games to be played. The Orange Game is one that will satisfy the players who must be doing something and at the same time it will delight the watchers. Pass the Matchbox is another of this type and certain forms of charades will accomplish the same thing.

You're the master mind behind this party and your main object is to keep everyone happy. You might as well admit to yourself from the very beginning that not everyone is going to be happy doing the same thing. Give the few something they want to see happen and the others something they want to do and you're pretty safe.

The secret combination lies in the selection of games. We've wrapped up two party packages, one of charades and its variations and one of general games. These are parties which have been successful with different groups of adults at different times. But there is no rule which says these are the only games you can play with large groups. The parties, as planned for eighty people, are merely intended to give you an idea of what you will need for each game and how games can be combined to fit one evening.

But whether you play these games or others, one thing is certain—if you and your committee plan the party carefully, if you gather all the necessary equipment before the party starts, and if you approach the whole thing with enthusiasm, yours will be the party the club remembers for a long time.

Charade Party

Tableau, Race Charades, and Paper Charades are all well adapted to large-scale playing and the three, combined with a starter game, make a perfect combination for one party. After the first explanations are over, you'll find the games practically play themselves. Your job will be to try and keep up with the guests.

Start the night off with The Spider Web (page 23). This will take about an hour's work on the part of the committee, but it is worth the effort because the game not only keeps those who arrive early busy but also serves as a way to establish teams. Instead of winding their strings on spools or cards in race fashion, the guests follow the strings to their team meeting points.

Once everyone has reached his team spot, distribute pencil and paper to each player and start Tableau (page 51). This is the point for committee members to get into the act, because instead of teams acting out tableaux for one another, the committee acts out a whole series of prearranged and rehearsed tableaux for the entire group to guess. Each tableau is held for only thirty seconds and then the committee relaxes from these positions and prepares for the next one. A small stage is ideal for this, but if your room doesn't have one any raised platform will do just as well, so long as it is large enough and strong enough to hold about five people at a time. Guests guess the tableaux by teams or individually, according to which seems the best for your party. The important thing is to prepare at least twenty tableaux and then present these well and fast. You might find that when the time comes to give the correct answer to each tableau, the guests will enjoy having the committee take their positions for each once more, so they can see what they might have missed the first time.

When played in this fashion, Tableau becomes a spectator game, which means that the guests will then be in the mood for the change of pace offered by Race Charades (page 48). Prepare the list of charades for this well ahead of time and make out many more than you think will be necessary. When a large group gets playing Race Charades, team competition runs high and the playing often goes faster and lasts longer than you had planned. Your charade list will have to be lengthy to keep up with the number of times the game is played.

Directions for playing Race Charades are long and somewhat complicated, because they should include the signals with which the actor helps his team guess. The demonstration technique mentioned earlier is helpful, but to some people the written word is the only one that counts. You'll save yourself a lot of breath and the guests a lot of bewilderment if you prepare a sheet which puts the whole thing in writing. That committee member you picked because of his mimeograph machine has come in handy along about now. And so has anyone who can make some simple line drawings. Combine with a few words on what each signal means and the playing coast should be perfectly clear.

With the direction sheets distributed, the game is then played as it would be in your home, with all teams acting out and guessing the same charades. But where in your home you need only one person with a list stationed at the midway point, you will now need four. Place four committee members at two card tables in the center of the floor. Each one has a list of the charades to be acted out, so that when a player races up to report the correct answer there is no delay in giving him the next problem.

Race Charades builds up team spirit and gets everyone ready for the more difficult version known as Paper Charades (page 49). For this you either provide each team with a standing blackboard and chalk or a pad of large, unlined paper, such as is used by artists and architects for sketching, and black crayon. As in Race Charades, players get the charades from a four-man committee in the center of the room, only this time, instead of acting, they must draw with chalk or crayon to make themselves clear to their teammates.

These four games, Spider Web, Tableau, Race Charades, and Paper Charades, are all you need for one evening, as each takes up quite a bit of playing time.

Old Clothes Party

This is a party designed for casual dress and informal fun. In fact, old clothes are a must, because some of the games are really active and one even gets people down on the floor. This is information you should pass along with the invitation or announcement.

You'll need a starter game. This can be Billboard (page 113), What's My Name? (page 10), or "When I Was a Child" (page 22). Very few changes are required to adapt these games for large groups. Billboard, as played in the house, requires twenty ads. Assuming you're planning a party for eighty, the number of ads should be increased to thirty. What's My Name? will take only more names of famous people, one for each guest. If you plan to use When I Was a Child, don't worry about getting each player's baby picture. Before the party gather about thirty baby or at least very early pictures of people you are sure will attend the party. This will be plenty for the guests to try to identify. Have this gallery set up ahead of time and have pencils and paper near the door so that those arriving early may start immediately.

Because it is quiet and played individually, What's My Name? or any of the other starter games should be followed by one which involves everyone at once, either as spectator or participant. Try something like the Streamer Race. Ten players on a team is the maximum for this. The ribbons or paper streamers have been cut to the proper length beforehand, so all you have to do is distribute the scissors and let the first team start cutting. Members of a team race against each other and then the winners from each team race to determine the final victor.

Under the Pole (page 133) is a game which lets everyone play in couples instead of larger teams. It is extremely active, but has a great advantage in that it combines good spectator appeal with actual participation. With a large group there is bound to be a long wait between the times it is a guest's turn to crawl under the pole, but the wait is spent in watching others struggle to do the same thing.

Good party sense says to follow this with a game which takes only one or two members from each team and leaves the others sitting and watching. Games good for this purpose are The Orange Game (page 54), Pass the Matchbox (page 57), and The Last Straw (page 57).

And then you come to the Horse Race. If you have a room of people who want to bet real money this is the game for them. But if you have guests who want to play just for the fun of it, the game has just as much appeal. Because it takes so much room, the Horse Race has not been described elsewhere in this book.

You will need: Chalk
Two dice, each of a different color
Pencils and paper for the people taking bets
6 teams

Chalk off 6 parallel lanes on the floor. These should be at least 20 feet long. Then divide each of these lanes into 20 boxes. Mark one end of the lanes as the starting line and the other end as the finish. Lanes are numbered from left to right.

One member from each team takes his place at the starting line for the first race and the other players place their bets. Whether you plan to play with money or only slips of paper, be kind to your committee members who are taking bets and limit all bets to win only, rather than place or show. Placing a paper bet is as simple as having guests go to the committee members who are stationed at several different tables and get a slip on which is written the number of the horse they want to win and the number of the race.

Regular dice may be used, or you may wish to construct some oversized ones which will be easier for everyone to see. Wooden dice, one foot square and painted with dots, are easy to make and add excitement to the game because they can be rolled on the floor at one end of the track. The dice must be of different colors. Assuming that one is red and one white, the red one indicates which horse should move and the white one the number of boxes he should advance. The rolling of the dice continues until a horse is across the finish line and becomes the winner for that race. Crossing the finish line requires an exact roll to fit the number of boxes still to be advanced. If, for example, a horse had three boxes still to go and the dice turned up with a 6, he could not move. It would have to be a 4 (one for each box and one to cross the finish line), or less than 4, before he could move. The dice may fall so that a horse gets right up to the finish line, but he has to stay in the last box until a 1 is rolled to get him across.

You may also decide to have a hurdle race. In this case it takes a roll of doubles to get a horse over a hurdle. Horse No. 3, for example, has to be rolled a 3 on the move dice before he can jump the hurdle. Hurdles are not essential, but they do even up the race a bit and give other horses a chance to catch up to what seemed a fast winner.

The game proceeds through as many races as you wish. For those who play with real money, there is no question as to the winner. For those playing with tickets, the person who has accumulated the most winning slips holds first prize.

The Horse Race not only takes time, but it also allows players a breathing spell, for while it is exciting, it is not energetic. Consequently, you'll find your guests are ready for one final fling in the form of a Full Dress Relay (page 128) or Musical Laps. This last game is nothing more than a variation of Musical Chairs, which takes only half the usual number of chairs and requires greater agility on the part of the players. Any number can play, but it is important to make sure that the total of men is one less than the total of women. Chairs are set up in the usual Musical Chairs fashion, the seat of the first facing in one direction, the seat of the second in the opposite direction, and so on until a chair has been placed for each man. The music starts and the guests move in a circle around the line of chairs. When the music stops, instead of just grabbing a chair, each girl must sit on the lap of a man who has already found himself a chair.

The girl who couldn't find herself a lap is eliminated and so is the chair and the man sitting on it from one of the ends. (Alternate the ends from which you take the chair). Play continues until at the end you have two girls, one man, and one chair. The couple landing in the chair are the winners.

Charts for Selecting Games

Chart 1. STARTER GAMES

GAME	PAGE	GAME	PAGE
Grab the Plate	15	Pardon My Pointing	15
Handshake	20	Profiles	21
How They Met	17	Shake the Penny	21
Identity	13	The Smelling Game	19
Match Book	22	Spider Web	23
Match Building	14	States and Cities	18
Name Game	17	What's My Name	10
Names	12	When I Was a Child	22
On My Left	16	Zoo	13
Overflow	22		

Chart 2. ACTIVE GAMES

GAME	PAGE	GAME	PAGE
Acting Rhymes	119	Get the Marshmallow	131
Alphabet Rhythm	86	Hoop-la	127
Applesauce	132	Horse Race	164
Balance the Egg	123	How Many	117
Balloon Volleyball	124	In the Air	126
The Big Stretch	130	Jail	129
Blow Fish	123	Leading the Blind	128
Card Flip	90	Line-up	127
Carry Your Chair	130	Murder	52
Charades	44	Musical Laps	165
Cracker Crumbs	132	Necktie Race	126
Eggshell Hockey	132	Number Game	114
Fizz Baseball	110	Number Relay	122
Fruit Relay	124	Olympics	125
Full Dress Relay	128	Paper Charades	49

Chart 3. QUIET GAMES

Chart 4. TRICK GAMES

Chart 5. HUNTS

Chart 6. GAMES THAT ARE FUN BUT FOOLISH

Chart 7. GAMES REQUIRING NO PRIOR PREPARATION

Chart 8. GAMES PLAYED WITH PENCIL AND PAPER

Chart 9. GAMES FOR SMALL GROUPS (2 to 8 Players)

Chart 10. GAMES FOR MEDIUM-SIZED GROUPS (8 to 12 Players)

Chart 11. GAMES FOR LARGE GROUPS
(More than 12 Players)

GAME	PAGE	GAME	PAGE
Acting Rhymes	119	Number Game	114
Alphabet Rhythm	86	Number Relay	122
Balance the Egg	123	Observation	108
Balloon Volleyball	124	Olympics	125
The Big Stretch	130	On My Left	16
Billboard	113	The Orange Game	54
Cahoots	65	Paper Charades	49
Camouflage	135	Pardon My Pointing	15
Carry Your Chair	130	Pass the Hot Potato	121
Charades	44	Pass the Matchbox	63
Cracker Crumbs	132	Peanuts	131
Crossed or Uncrossed?	69	Pin Boy	125
Eggshell Hockey	132	Ping Pong Basketball	89
Expert	32	Poker Face	60
Fifty-six	88	Profiles	21
Fizz Baseball	110	Proverbs	107
Fruit Relay	124	Quiz Program	93
Full Dress Relay	128	Race Charades	48
Get the Marshmallow	131	Rogues' Gallery	106
Grab the Plate	15	Sew a Button	90
Hall of Fame	25	Shake the Penny	21
Handshake	20	Sight Unseen	50
Hoop-la	127	Simple Treasure Hunt	140
Horse Race	164	The Smelling Game	19
How Many?	117	Spider Web	23
Identity	17	Sportsman's Row	115
Indoor Scavenger Hunt	138	States and Cities	18
In the Air	126	Streamer Race	129
Jail	129	Tableau	51
The Last Straw	57	Take a Base	91
Leading the Blind	128	Test Kitchen	85
Letter Hunt	137	This Is My Nose	107
Line-up	127	Three Matches	43
Match Building	14	Three of a Kind	76
Murder	52	Three W's	33
Musical Laps	165	Tree Leaves	109
My Bequest	61	Twenty-five Letters	24
Name Game	17	Under the Pole	133
Names	12	Up, Jenkins	87
Name Your City	30	Upside Down Scavenger Hunt	137
Necktie Race	126		

GAME	PAGE	GAME	PAGE
Ventriloquist	59	What's the Scoop?	118
What Dropped?	116	When I Was a Child	22
What Is a Mugwump?	58	Word Building	29
What Is It?	104	Word Factory	33
What's My Name?	10	Word Rhymes	120
What's the City?	72	Words and Pictures	92
What's the Product?	112	Zoo	13

Chart 12. GAMES THAT TAKE ABOUT 15 MINUTES

GAME	PAGE	GAME	PAGE
Applesauce	132	Nine Squares	83
Automobile Show	70	Observation	108
Balance the Egg	123	Odd or Even?	84
The Barnyard	78	Olympics	125
The Big Stretch	130	Overflow	22
Blow Fish	123	Pardon My Pointing	15
Car Lot	28	Pass the Hot Potato	121
Card Flip	90	Pass the Matchbox	63
Concentrate	77	Peanuts	131
Copy Cat	79	Pin Boy	125
Cracker Crumbs	132	Pinchy Winchy	55
Crossed or Uncrossed?	69	Poker Face	60
Eggshell Hockey	132	Proverb Ball	36
The Fingerprint	78	Psychic	77
Grab the Plate	15	Rogues' Gallery	106
Handshake	20	Signature	64
He Can Do Little	72	Sportsman's Row	115
Hoop-la	127	Stick Pin	89
How Many?	117	Sticky Dime	75
I Am Going to Duluth	126	This Is My Nose	107
Identity	17	Three of a Kind	76
In the Air	126	Tilly Williams	55
Jail	129	Tree Leaves	109
The Jigger Trick	82	Up, Jenkins	87
Laughter to Tears	60	What Time Is It?	76
Leading the Blind	128	Where's the Nickel?	83
Line-up	127	Who's the Owner?	69
Match Book	22	Word Building	29
My Grandmother's Trunk	111	Your Favorite Object	62
Names	12	Zoo	13
Necktie Race	126		

Chart 13. GAMES THAT TAKE ABOUT 30 TO 45 MINUTES

GAME	PAGE
Acting Rhymes	119
Alphabet Rhythm	86
Balloon Volleyball	124
The Berries	70
Billboard	113
Bird, Fish, or Animal?	26
Cahoots	65
Camouflage	135
Carry Your Chair	130
The Circle	75
Cootie	92
Expert	32
Famous People	39
Fifty-six	88
Five Coins	82
Five Glasses	81
Five in a Row	67
Fizz Baseball	110
Forbidden Letter	103
From A to Z	29
From One to Fifty	74
Fruit Relay	124
Full Dress Relay	128
Get the Marshmallow	131
Going to Europe	63
Good Guess	67
Guggenheim	26
Hall of Fame	25
Hangman	40
How They Met	105
Indoor Scavenger Hunt	138
The Last Straw	57
Letter Hunt	137
Magic Touch	73
Match Building	14
Match Jump	79
Match Squares	80
Match Triangles	81
Memory Lane	28
Musical Laps	165
My Bequest	61
My Grandmother	56
Name Game	17
Name Your City	30
Nine Books	68
Nine to Ten	80
No, It's Not	34
Number Game	114
Number Relay	122
On My Left	16
Our Cook Doesn't Like Peas	56
Pick a Number	74
Ping Pong Basketball	89
Predicament	60
Profiles	21
Proverbs	107
Quiz Program	93
Radar	71
Rogues' Gallery	106
Shake the Penny	21
Sight Unseen	50
Simple Treasure Hunt	140
The Smelling Game	19
Spider Web	23
States and Cities	18
Streamer Race	129
Take a Base	91
Teapot	41
Test Kitchen	85
That's It	73
This or That?	66
Three Guesses	38
Three Matches	43
Three Words	115
Three W's	33
Twenty-five Letters	24
Under the Pole	133
Upside Down Scavenger Hunt	137
Ventriloquist	59
Vocabulary	26

GAME	PAGE	GAME	PAGE
What Dropped?	116	What's the Scoop?	118
What Is It?	104	When I Was a Child	22
What's a Mugwump?	58	Word Factory	33
What's My Name?	10	Word Relations	31
What's the City?	72	Word Rhymes	120
What's the Product?	112	Words and Pictures	92
What's the Proverb?	35		

Chart 14. GAMES THAT TAKE ONE HOUR TO AN EVENING

GAME	PAGE	GAME	PAGE
Charades	44	Race Charades	48
Horse Race	164	Tableau	51
Murder	52	Temp's Treasure Hunt	140
Paper Charades	49		